Talk About the Cover

Roadrunner

Roadrunner, roadrunner, you can RUN

Through the desert just for **FUN**.

Faster than the *WIND* can blow,

Roadrunner, roadrunner, off you GO!

How fast can YOU run?

ISBN 0-15-334264-1

3 4 5 6 7 8 9 10   030   10 09 08 07 06 05 04

Moving into English

Authors

Alma Flor Ada • F. Isabel Campoy • Yolanda N. Padrón • Nancy Roser

Harcourt

Orlando   Austin   Chicago   New York   Toronto   London   San Diego

Visit *The Learning Site!*
www.harcourtschool.com

UNIT 1 SELF-DISCOVERY

Self-Discovery

Review Vocabulary with a Play

STORIES ON STAGE

CONTENTS

Working Together

Review Vocabulary with a Play
★ STORIES ON STAGE ★

CONTENTS

Growth and Change

Review Vocabulary with a Play

★ STORIES ON STAGE ★

4

CONTENTS

Creativity

Review Vocabulary with a Play

★ STORIES ON STAGE ★

CONTENTS

Communities

CONTENTS

Explorations

Review Vocabulary with a Play
★ STORIES ON STAGE ★

Use What You Know

Bonsai trees are like regular trees, but they grow no higher than a person's knee. To make a bonsai, a gardener puts a young tree in a very small container instead of in the ground. In the container, a bonsai's roots can't grow very far. The gardener also can control the size of the tree by cutting back the roots.

■ **Use prior knowledge**

"A bonsai tree must look like a regular tree, only smaller."

■ **Think about expressions**

"I think *no higher* means the same as *no taller.*"

■ **Reason**

"A bonsai tree can be as beautiful as a regular tree and take up less space."

8

Find Help

Mammoth Cave National Park in Kentucky has the longest known cave system in the world. It is about 348 miles long and 379 feet deep. There are more than seventy threatened or endangered species living in the park. Many of these plants and animals could not live in other places because they have adapted to life in a cave environment.

■ **Use a computer**

"I can look for a map of Kentucky on the Internet."

■ **Ask for help**

"I can ask my teacher or a friend how to say *species.*"

■ **Use books**

"The dictionary says that to adapt is to change because of conditions."

Make Connections

Antarctica is an interesting place to study because of its very cold climate. Scientists have discovered that fish can survive in Antarctica's icy waters because their blood contains a kind of antifreeze. On the surface of Antarctica, scientists have found thousands of rocks from outer space. Scientists also have discovered that several lakes lie beneath Antarctica.

■ **Use word structure**

"The prefix *anti-* means the same as *not*. Antifreeze must be something that does *not* freeze."

■ **Compare and contrast**

"Antarctica is mostly cold and snowy, but Florida is sunny and warm."

■ **Use maps and charts**

"Antarctica covers the South Pole. Maybe that is why it's so cold."

Picture It

Every summer my younger sister and I visit our grandparents in Colorado. They have a small farm, and we help them with the chores while we're there. Every morning it's my job to feed the animals and to gather eggs for breakfast. My sister and I also groom and exercise our grandparents' horses. Taking care of the horses is our favorite chore.

■ **Describe it**

"To help me remember the events, I describe the chores to a classmate."

■ **Memorize**

"I pick out important words that describe the subject. Then I create a word web to help me remember them."

■ **Use actions**

"I think about how the children would complete their chores. I act out how I think they would do them."

11

Look for Patterns

■ **Use repetition**

Lines 2, 4, 6, and 8 have a pattern.

■ **Think about words and phrases**

"I think *splish-splash* tells me the sound that the sea makes when the tree falls in."

■ **Use text structure**

The first eight lines include *sea, tree, axe,* and *man.* The last four lines repeat those words, but in reverse order.

If all the seas were one sea,
What a *great* sea that would be!
If all the trees were one tree,
What a *great* tree that would be!
And if all the axes were one axe,
What a *great* axe that would be!
And if all the men were one man,
What a *great* man that would be!
And if the *great* man took the *great* axe,
And cut down the *great* tree,
And let it fall into the *great* sea,
What a splish-splash that would be!

Set a Purpose

Paper products, glass bottles, plastic bags, and aluminum cans are all items that can be recycled. By recycling, you can conserve natural resources and preserve the Earth for people in the future. Recycling also saves money for both you and your city.

- **Purpose for listening**

  "I will listen to find out what I can recycle."

- **Purpose for speaking**

  "I want to talk with my classmates about starting a recycling program at our school."

- **Purpose for reading**

  "I want to find out why people should recycle."

- **Purpose for writing**

  "I want to write a report about the materials that can be recycled."

13

globe

journal

drawer

14

ctionary

SING ALONG

About Me

I'm learning more about myself
And what things make me special.
Self–discovery,
Self–discovery,
Self–discovery
I'm learning why I'm special!

*Sing to the tune of
"Bingo."*

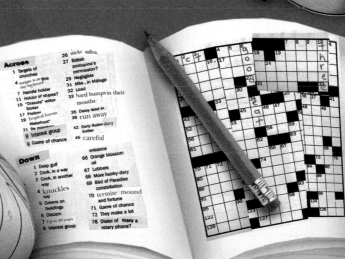

Narrative Elements: Plot

The **plot** is what happens in a story. In most stories, the main character has a problem. The plot shows how the character solves the problem.

Read the paragraph. Then look at the chart to see the problem and the solution.

The Riveras are going on vacation, but they can't decide where to go. Mrs. Rivera gets out a map of the United States. She asks her son José to close his eyes and put his finger on a spot on the map. José puts his finger on Arizona. The Riveras are going to Arizona to see the Grand Canyon.

Plot	
Problem	**Solution**
The Riveras can't decide where to go on vacation.	Mrs. Rivera asks her son to put his finger on a spot on the map.

Try This

▶ Read the paragraph. Then copy the chart onto a separate
sheet of paper. Use the information in the paragraph to
complete the chart.

Wendy is afraid to put her head under the water at
the pool. Coach Norman teaches her a trick. "Keep
one hand in the air while
your face is under the water,"
he says. "It will help you
relax." Wendy tries the trick,
and it works!

Plot	
Problem	**Solution**

Vocabulary POWER

Nico's Trip ▼

VOCABULARY

nervous

trip

parents

hungry

airport

team

neighborhood

plane

My family and I took a long car **trip** last summer.

This man is waiting at the **airport**. Soon he will get on the **plane**.

I play on a baseball **team**. I was **nervous** before the game started, but now I'm having fun.

This is my favorite picture of my **parents** and me.

Mr. and Mrs. Smith were very **hungry** by the time the food arrived.

The houses in my **neighborhood** look small from a plane.

NICO'S TRIP

TICKET

My name is Nico. I am 11 years old, and I live in Mexico. This is the story of my first trip to the United States.

Monday, August 11

Today was my first day in the United States! The plane ride was fun, but it was long. I was nervous about meeting my cousin, Melina, even though my parents said I would like her.

Melina, Uncle Juan, and Aunt Susan met me at the airport. Uncle Juan and Aunt Susan seemed happy to see me. Melina didn't say much. I was quiet, too.

When we got to Uncle Juan and Aunt Susan's house, the first thing I did was to call my mother and father. I told them about the plane trip and said that I was fine.

Tuesday, August 12

I was tired from yesterday's plane ride. I slept until noon!

My aunt and uncle live in a quiet neighborhood with a lot of trees. Their house is large, and I can see the backyard from the window in my room.

Before dinner Melina taught me some new English words. Dinner was ready very early—at 6:00. I wasn't very hungry, but the grilled steak and green beans Uncle Juan cooked smelled so delicious that I ate them anyway.

Wednesday, August 13

Aunt Susan and I left the house early in the morning. We went to a soccer game, and Melina was there with her team. We both play soccer! I was surprised to find out how much we have in common.

The game was exciting. I cheered very loudly. Near the end of the game, Melina made a goal, and her team won. She was really happy, and so was I. She even gave me the soccer ball as a present.

After the game, I met Melina's friends. They were very nice and asked me all about Mexico and my family. I told them about the soccer team I play on in Mexico.

Later, Melina told me more about her soccer team. She said her team is very good this year. She thinks it's going to win the championship. I agree!

Thursday, August 14

Today was another special day. The weather was very warm. Bright sunshine came in the kitchen window while we were eating breakfast. Melina helped Aunt Susan make pancakes. Because I am a guest, they served me extra strawberries. My mother called in the middle of breakfast to say hello. She spoke with everyone, including Melina. I didn't know Melina could speak Spanish so well.

After breakfast we went to the beach. The sand was so hot that it burned my feet. Uncle Juan and Aunt Susan sat on a blanket, and Melina ran into the ocean. I felt the water, and it was very cold. The water at the beach in Mexico is much warmer. I finally decided to go swimming, and I discovered that swimming in cold water can be nice. It cools you off on a hot day.

Friday, August 15

Today we had a picnic in the park. Well, we *tried* to have a picnic. I took the soccer ball Melina had given me. We had fun kicking the ball around. When we sat down to have lunch, it began to rain. We went back to the house to eat lunch. While we were eating, Aunt Susan suggested that we go see a movie in the city. What a great idea!

At the movie theater, Uncle Juan bought popcorn and sodas for all of us. We saw a science fiction movie. It was exciting! Aunt Susan said she likes love stories better, just like my mother.

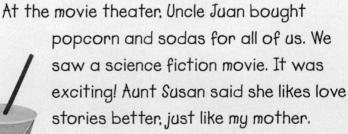

Saturday, August 16

Today after dinner Aunt Susan said that since this was the last night of my vacation, we were going to toast marshmallows as a treat. I said I had never seen a marshmallow.

Melina brought out a bag filled with soft, spongy white things. She pushed a stick through one of them and held it over the fire. I did the same. The marshmallows soon toasted and turned brown. They also became very hot. I waited for mine to cool off before I tasted it. Wow! Toasted marshmallows are delicious! Inside the brown part, they're sticky and sweet.

We stayed up late talking around the fire. It was a quiet night. We could hear only ourselves talking and the crickets chirping. Later, back in my room, I thought about all the things we had done. I felt a little sad. I always feel sad about saying good-bye.

Sunday, August 17

This was my last day in the United States. The week went by quickly, but I have many stories to tell! Part of me was happy to go back home because I missed my parents and my friends. I know I am going to miss my aunt and uncle and especially Melina.

Uncle Juan, Aunt Susan, and Melina all took me to the airport. We drove through the city, and I recognized some of the buildings and streets. The theater was still showing the movie we saw. The airport seemed smaller this time, maybe because I had been there before.

Uncle Juan hugged me tightly. Aunt Susan's eyes became big and red. I think she told me a hundred times to have a safe trip. I promised Melina that I would e-mail her soon.

Melina gave me a big hug and said she was going to miss me. Uncle Juan gave me a picture of the four of us. I keep it here, safe between the pages of this diary.

I'm writing this at home in my own room. On the shelf above my desk is the soccer ball Melina gave me. I will look at it every day and remember all the things I learned about in the United States. My favorite one? I know that I will never forget the smell of toasted marshmallows.

Think Critically

❶ What did Nico do during his trip to the United States? What new things did he learn about?

❷ How did Nico feel about his trip at the beginning? How did his feelings change?

❸ How does Nico feel when he learns that Melina plays on a soccer team?

❹ Would you like to take a trip to a different country? Explain your answer.

My Place on the Map ▼

VOCABULARY

country

state

ocean

cattle

island

beach

climates

mountains

The **state** of Texas is very large. People raise many **cattle** there.

My family and I like to go to the **beach** on warm, sunny days.

28

We climbed high into the **mountains**.

In the large **ocean**, the rocky **island** looked very small.

Our **country**, the United States, has many **climates**—some mostly cold and some mostly hot.

My Place on the Map

There are many kinds of regions in the United States. In this selection, three young people in different parts of the country will tell about the places where they live. As you read, think about how these three regions are like or unlike your own.

Jonesport, Maine

My name is Kevin. I live in Jonesport, a village on the coast of Maine. It's a great place to live!

The state of Maine is on the east coast of the United States. The ocean is an important part of Maine's history and economy. In my town almost everyone's work is connected with the ocean. Some of my neighbors are fishermen. My father catches and sells lobsters. About half of the lobsters sold in this country come from Maine.

Young people who want to learn how to catch lobsters start by helping one of the catchers in the village.

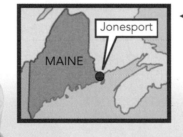

◀ **Maine has a beautiful coast, lakes, mountains, and forests.**

Houston, Texas

My name is Tom, and I live in Texas. My parents own a cattle ranch. Cattle ranching has been an important business in Texas for nearly 300 years. Today Texas raises more cattle than any other state in the country.

People say that "everything is big in Texas." My family's ranch covers more than one and a half square miles! Some Texas ranches are much bigger. It can take half a day just to get across them on horseback!

On a ranch the cattle usually are left by themselves to graze on the land. Sometimes, though, the cowhands ride their horses to gather the cattle. This is called a roundup.

Special clothing helps ▶
cowhands do their jobs.

Large areas of open land, or range, make ▶
Texas a good place to raise cattle.

TEXAS

Houston

Roundups take place when the cows have their babies, or calves, and again when the calves are old enough to leave their mothers.

Cowhands still ride horses, but they also use tractors and other machines in their work. On really big ranches, cowhands sometimes use helicopters at roundup time.

Cowhands wear big hats that protect them from the hot sun and wet weather. Cowhands wear special boots for a reason, too. The pointed toes make them easier to slip into the stirrups that hang from a horse's saddle.

Life on a ranch is fun. I help look after the horses and cattle. It can be hard work, but I love it!

Oahu, Hawaii

My name is Cindy, and I live on the island of Oahu in the state of Hawaii.

Hawaii is made up of eight main islands and many smaller ones. The first Hawaiians probably came from Polynesia, in the South Pacific.

Hawaii has beautiful coral reefs. Corals are tiny animals that need clean, clear water and sunlight to live. A coral reef is made of the parts of corals that grow together.

HAWAII

Oahu

Coral reefs are home to many living things. By taking care of the reefs, we take care of all the plants and animals that live there.

Where I live, near the beach, it's warm and sunny even in the winter. Hawaii has other climates, though. Its islands are really the tops of volcanoes. If you travel from the base of one of the mountains to the top, you will find sunny beaches, tropical rain forests, cool mountain regions, and stony deserts. There are many different climates in Hawaii.

I think I'm lucky to live in Hawaii!

▼ **Oahu has more than 100 beaches, including some of Hawaii's best surfing beaches.**

Symbols

horseback riders crossing

railroad crossing

hospital

36

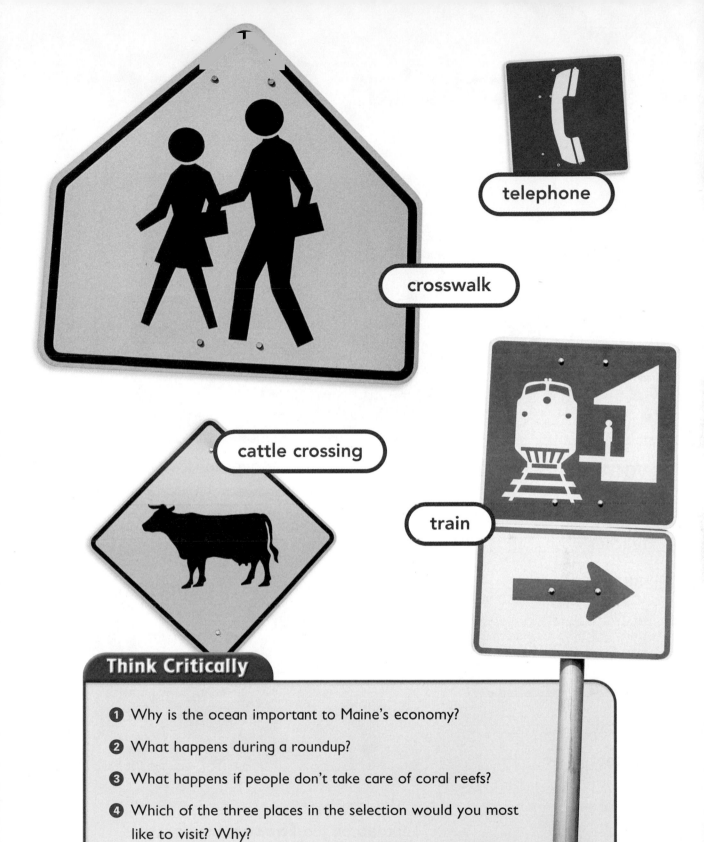

telephone

crosswalk

cattle crossing

train

Think Critically

1. Why is the ocean important to Maine's economy?

2. What happens during a roundup?

3. What happens if people don't take care of coral reefs?

4. Which of the three places in the selection would you most like to visit? Why?

Vocabulary POWER

Me-First Millie ▼

VOCABULARY

pencils

teacher

nurse

brave

shocked

warned

rushed

faucet

The **teacher** read the questions. The students marked the answers with their **pencils**.

I turned on the **faucet**, but no water came out.

38

The **brave** firefighter ran into the burning building. He **rushed** out with the child.

A **nurse** told our class about her job helping people who are sick.

The sign **warned** drivers to watch for animals crossing the road.

The actors looked **shocked** by what they saw.

Me-First Millie

by M. Donnaleen Howitt

When pencils were passed,
Or when plays were rehearsed,
One voice could be heard
Yelling, "Me! I'll be first!"

"Millie, dear," said the teacher,
"Someday you must learn
To wait like the others
And take your fair turn."

The children lined up
In a neat little row.
"Look out!" shouted Justin,
"You stepped on my toe!"

Millie pushed to the front
With her lips firmly pursed.
She didn't say, "Sorry."
She just said, "Me first!"

At lunchtime, poor Rita
Was lined up to pay,
When Millie-Me-First
Bumped her hard with her tray.

At playtime, that Millie
Was sure at her worst!
She grabbed every ball
And said, "Let me go first!"

Soon all of the children
Stepped out of the way
And let Millie lead
In the lessons and play.

One day there were papers
For mothers to sign
And send back to school
With their names on the line.

"Line up," said the teacher,
"At Nurse Murphy's door.
Please hand her your papers.
You'll see what they're for."

"Me first!" shouted Millie.
Nurse Murphy said, "Fine!
A brave little girl
At the head of the line!"

She held Millie's arm
(It was time for a shot),
And Millie was shocked
At the poke that she got!

"We're studying Mexico!"
The teacher declared.
"We'll have quite a feast
When the food is all shared."

José brought some peppers
And warned they were hot.
But too late for Millie,
Who was first at the pot.

Her mouth was on fire,
And tears filled her eyes.
She never expected
That red-hot surprise!

At home, Millie rushed
To be first in the shower.
Her brother was sure
She'd be there for an hour.

He rapped on the door
And yelled through the lock,
"The water is cold,
And you're in for a shock!"

Poor Millie was gasping
And shivering too.
She reached for the faucet
And nearly turned blue!

Now Millie was smart,
And it didn't take long
To think and to figure
Just what had gone wrong.

From then on she stood
At the end of the line
And said, "After you.
Why, the pleasure's all mine!"

The kids were surprised
And delighted to see
That Millie could act
Just as nice as could be.

For Millie had learned,
(As the others had done)
You don't have to be first
To be called "Number One"!

Think Critically

❶ What bad things happen to Millie because she always wants
to be first?

❷ What does Millie learn?

❸ How do you think Millie has changed from the beginning of the poem?

❹ Would you like to be friends with Millie? Why or why not?

Vocabulary POWER

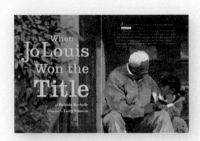

My **grandfather** grew up in a very small town. He went to **school** in a one-room building.

Thanksgiving is a holiday in November. Many families celebrate by having a **special** meal.

The **train** carries the farmers' crops to the city.

The student raised her hand to ask a **question**.

Taxis hurry through the **streets**. They help people move around in the **city**.

Each student has a basket with his or her **name** on it.

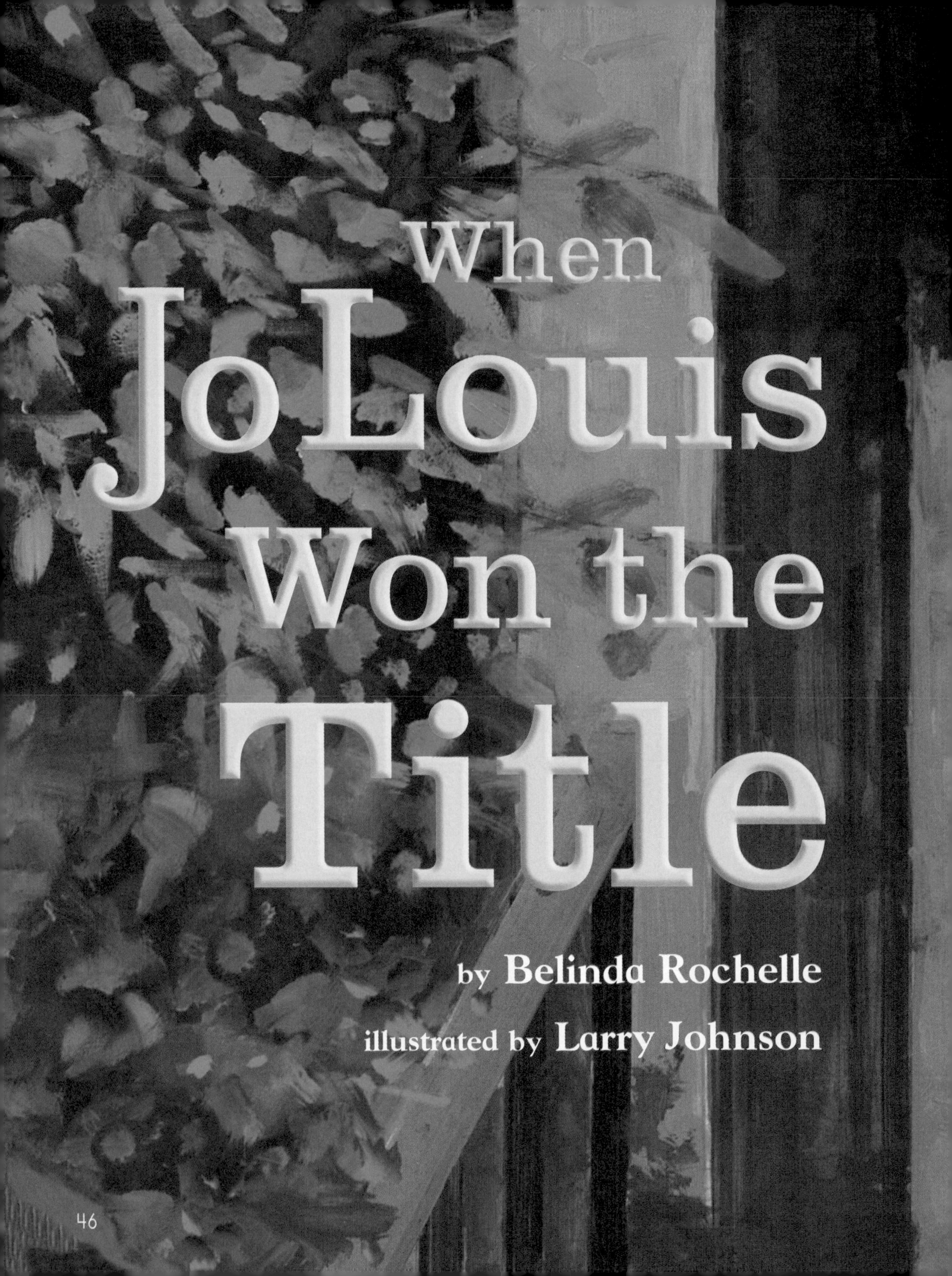

When JoLouis Won the Title

by **Belinda Rochelle**

illustrated by **Larry Johnson**

Jo Louis sat perched on the top step of ten steps, waiting for her grandfather, John Henry.

"Is that my favorite girl in the whole wide world?" he said as he strolled up the street. He leaned over and picked up Jo Louis, swung her round and round until her ponytails whirled like the propellers of a plane, swung her round and round until they were both dizzy with gasps, swung her round and round until they were both dizzy with giggles.

John Henry's brown eyes twinkled as he returned Jo Louis to the top step and sat down next to her. The smile quickly disappeared from Jo Louis's face. "Why such a sad face on a pretty girl?" he asked.

Tomorrow was a special day for Jo Louis. The first day at a new school.

"I don't want to go to school!" Jo Louis said to her grandfather. "I don't want to be the new girl in a new neighborhood at a new school."

John Henry put his arm around her and pulled her close.

"Why don't you want to go to school?" he asked.

"I'll probably be the shortest kid in class, or I'll be the one who can't run as fast as the other kids. I finish every race last."

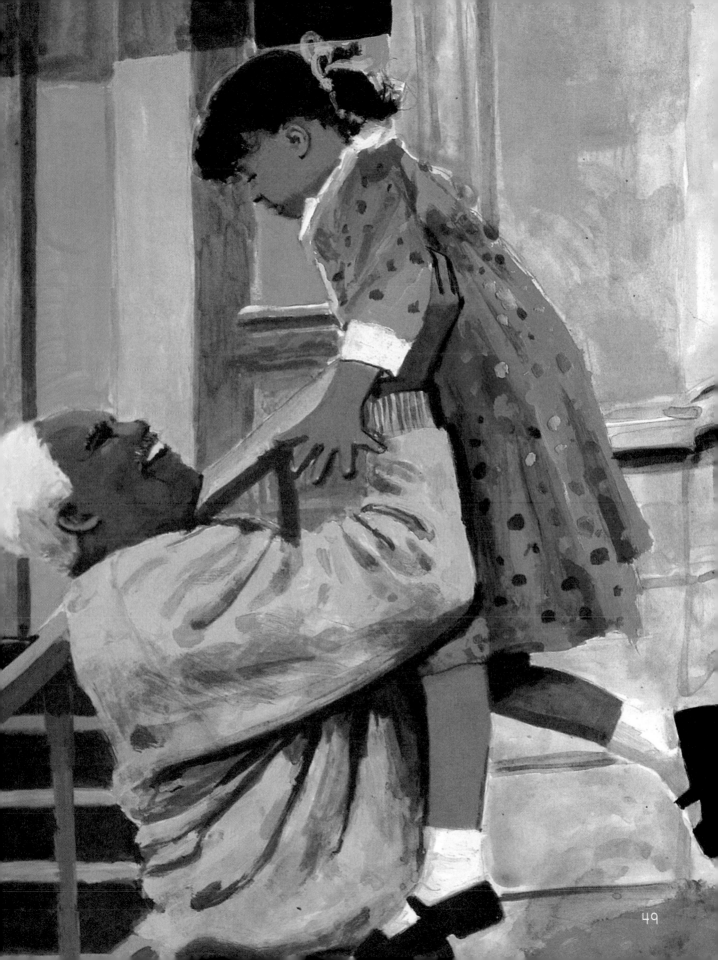

"It's just a matter of time before a new school is an old school. Just a matter of time before you'll be able to run really fast, and you won't always finish last," he said, patting her hand. "What's the real reason you don't want to go to school?" John Henry asked.

Jo Louis shook her head. It was hard to explain. She just knew it would happen. Someone would ask THE question. IT was THE question, the same question each and every time she met someone new: *"What's your name?"*

It was that moment, that question, that made Jo Louis want to disappear. And it really wouldn't make a difference if she were taller, and it wouldn't make a difference that she was the new kid in school, and it wouldn't make a difference if she could run really fast. She just wished that she didn't have to tell anyone her name.

Her grandfather picked her up and placed her on his knee. "Let me tell you a story," he said.

"When I was just a young boy living in Mississippi," he began, "I used to dream about moving north. To me it was the promised land. I wanted to find a good job in the big city. Cities like Chicago, St. Louis. But everybody, I mean everybody, talked about Harlem in New York City. Going north, it was all anybody ever talked about. I would sit on the front porch and just daydream about those big-city places. The way some folks told it everything was perfect. Even the streets in the big city were paved with gold, and it was all there just waiting for me."

John Henry's eyes sparkled as his voice quickened. "When I saved enough money, I crowded onto the train with other small-town folks headed north. Everything I owned fit into a torn, tattered suitcase and a brown box wrapped in string.

"I rode the train all day and all night. Like a snake winding its way across the Mississippi River, that train moved slowly through farmlands and flatland, over mountains and valleys, until it reached its final destination."

Jo Louis closed her eyes. She loved her grandfather's stories—his words were like wings and other things. She listened closely until she felt she was right there with him.

"'New York City! New York! New York!' the
conductor bellowed as the train pulled into the station.

"I headed straight to Harlem. I had never seen
buildings so tall. They almost seemed to touch the sky.
Even the moon looked different in the big city. The
moonlight was bright and shining, the stars skipped
across the sky.

"The streets sparkled in the night sky's light. It was true! The streets did seem to be paved in gold! I walked up and down city streets that stretched wide and long. I walked past a fancy nightclub, where you could hear the moaning of a saxophone and a woman singing so sad, so soft, and so slow that the music made me long for home.

And then, all of a sudden the sad music changed to happy music. That saxophone and singing started to swing. Hundreds of people spilled out into the sidewalks, waving flags, scarves, waving handkerchiefs and tablecloths. Hundreds of people filled the streets with noise and laughter, waving hats and anything and everything, filling the sky with bright colors of red, white, green, yellow, blue, purple, and orange.

"Everybody was clapping, hands were raised high to the sky. Up and down the street, people were shouting and singing. Cars were beeping their horns; bells were ringing.

"'Excuse me.' I patted a woman on the shoulder. 'What's going on?' I asked.

The woman smiled. She was pretty with soft, brown hair and a friendly smile. 'Why, haven't you heard?' she said, 'Joe Louis won the title fight. My name is Mary'—she held out her hand—'and your name is . . . ?'"

John Henry smiled and hugged Jo Louis close. "It was a special night for me. It was a special night for black people everywhere. Joe Louis was the greatest boxer in the world. He was a hero. That night he won the fight of his life. A fight that a lot of people thought he would lose. Some folks said he was too slow, others said he wasn't strong enough. But he worked hard and won. It was a special night, my first night in the big city, and Joe Louis won the fight. But the night was special for another reason."

"It was the night you met Grandma," Jo Louis said, and she started to smile.

"It was a special night that I'll never forget. I named your father Joe Louis, and he named you, his first child, Jo Louis, too." Her grandfather tickled her nose. "That was the night you won the title. You should be very proud of your name. Every name has a special story."

The next day Jo Louis took a deep breath as she walked into her new school classroom and slipped into a seat. The boy sitting next to Jo Louis tapped her on the shoulder. "My name is Lester. What's your name?"

Jo answered slowly, "My name is Jo . . . Jo Louis." She balled her fist and closed her eyes and braced herself. She waited, waited for the laughter, waited for the jokes. She peeked out of one eye, then she peeked out the other eye.

"Wow, what a great name!" he said, and smiled.

At School

music room

Welcome To
COVERY MIDDLE SCHOOL

playground

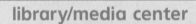
classroom

gym

library/media center

Think Critically

1. Why is Jo Louis sad at the beginning of the story?

2. Who is the pretty woman in the story? Why is she important?

3. Who is Jo Louis named for?

4. How do you think Jo Louis feels about her name at the end of the story? Why?

Review Vocabulary with a Play

STORIES ON STAGE

The Statue in Town Park

Review

VOCABULARY

grandfather

teacher

country

state

trip

parents

school

CHARACTERS

Carla Santiago, 10 years old

Jimmy Jee, Carla's classmate, 10 years old

Mr. Santiago, Carla's grandfather

Mr. Ritter, Carla and Jimmy's teacher

Ms. Stein, librarian

Mayor Brown, mayor of the town

Mrs. Jee, Jimmy's mother

Narrator

Scene 1

Setting: Friday afternoon in the classroom

Mr. Ritter: We've already learned about our country and our state. Now it's time to learn about our town. What do you know about our town?

Carla: There's a big statue in Town Park. It shows a man holding flowers.

Mr. Ritter: Do you know who the man with the flowers was?

Carla: Was he the person who started our town?

Mr. Ritter: No, but he lived here a long time ago.

Jimmy: Was he the first gardener? He *is* holding flowers.

Mr. Ritter: No, Jimmy, but those are good guesses. Students, I'd like you to find out about the statue. There's an interesting story connected with it!

Jimmy: Let's work on this together, Carla. My mother can take us to the library tomorrow.

Narrator: The students leave the classroom.

Scene 2

Setting: Saturday morning at Carla's house

Narrator: Jimmy enters Carla's house with his mother.

Jimmy: Hello, Mr. Santiago! Hi, Carla! Are you ready to go?

Carla: I'm ready. Hello, Mrs. Jee. Thank you for taking us to the library.

Mrs. Jee: You're welcome. I like learning new things about our town.

Mr. Santiago: Why are you going to the library?

Carla: We have to find out about the statue in Town Park.

Mr. Santiago: Is it the statue of the man holding flowers?

Jimmy: Yes, that's the statue.

Mr. Santiago: I grew up in this town. What do you want to know about the statue? Can I help?

Carla: Thanks, Grandpa, but we need to get going.

Jimmy and Mrs. Jee: Good-bye, Mr. Santiago.

Narrator: Jimmy, Mrs. Jee, and Carla go to the library.

Scene 3

Setting: At the public library

Narrator: Ms. Stein is putting some books on a shelf at the library. Jimmy and Carla walk in with Mrs. Jee.

Ms. Stein: Good morning! Can I help you?

Jimmy: Yes, please. We need help to find out about the statue in Town Park.

Carla: We need to find out who the man was that the statue honors. He must have been very important.

Ms. Stein: I'm sure you're right, but we don't have any books about the statue.

Jimmy: Could we check the old newspapers?

Ms. Stein: I'm sorry, but all the old newspapers burned in a fire years ago. That statue is very old. I did hear that there's an interesting story behind it.

Mrs. Jee: Maybe we should go to the park and look at the statue.

Jimmy: Good idea, Mom. We might find some clues there.

Scene 4

Setting: In Town Park

Narrator: Carla, Jimmy, and Mrs. Jee see Mr. Ritter and Mayor Brown in the park.

Carla: Hi, Mr. Ritter! What are you doing here?

Mr. Ritter: I come here every weekend to play chess with Mayor Brown.

Mayor Brown: Hello! What are you doing here?

Jimmy: We're trying to learn about the statue of the man holding flowers.

Mayor Brown: There's a story about it.

Mrs. Jee: Do you know the story, Mayor Brown?

Mayor Brown: No, but I know someone who does. It's someone who grew up in this town.

Mr. Ritter: And you know him very well, Carla.

Carla: Oh! It's Grandpa! He knows the story!

Jimmy: Let's go ask your grandfather!

Scene 5

Setting: Carla's house

Mr. Santiago: You're back. Did you find out about the statue?

Carla: No, but we found out that you could tell us about it!

Jimmy: Did you know the man holding the flowers?

Mr. Santiago: Yes, he was my father! My mother's family lived in this town. My father came here on a trip from another state. When he saw my mother, he fell in love with her.

Carla: What happened then, Grandpa?

Mr. Santiago: He stood in front of her house, holding flowers. Her parents said that he looked like a statue!

Carla: What did your mother do?

Mr. Santiago: She fell in love with him and they were married.

Mrs. Jee: What about the statue?

Mr. Santiago: For a wedding gift, her family had a real statue made to honor his love for their daughter.

Jimmy: What a great story for a play!

Carla: Let's ask Mr. Ritter if we can perform it in school!

Review Activities

Think and Respond

1 What are some things you have discovered about yourself while reading this unit?

2 Do you think Nico would want to return to the United States one day? Why or why not?

3 Which of the places you read about in "My Place on the Map" do you think is the most interesting? Why?

4 What does Millie learn about always being first?

5 What does Jo Louis discover about her name?

LANGUAGE STRUCTURE REVIEW

Make Introductions

Find out some information about a partner. Ask questions such as

- What is your full name?
- How old are you?
- Where were you born?
- What do you like to do?

Write down the information about your partner. Then introduce your partner to your classmates. Tell them your partner's name, age, where he or she was born, and what things he or she likes to do.

About Jorge

This is Jorge Martínez Esparza.

Jorge is ten years old. He was born in Mexico. Jorge likes to swim and play basketball.

VOCABULARY REVIEW

Draw That Word

Form two teams. Place the Vocabulary Cards from this unit face down in a pile.

Classmates on each team will take turns. When it's your turn, pick a Vocabulary Card from the pile. On the Dry-erase Board, draw picture clues about this word. Show your picture clues to your teammates. They will try to guess your word. When a teammate guesses the right word, that person has to use the word in a sentence. If the sentence is correct, your team gets a point. Then it's the other team's turn to play. The team with more points at the end of the game wins.

basketball

team

hoop

72

SING ALONG

Teamwork

Work, work, as a team—
Then you will succeed.
Teamwork and cooperation
Are just what you need.

Work, work in a group—
A job for everyone.
Planning, taking part, and sharing
Get the project done!

*Sing to the tune of
"Row, Row, Row Your Boat."*

Main Idea and Supporting Details

The **main idea** of a selection is what the selection is mostly about. The **supporting details** give more information about the main idea. The main idea is not always stated. If it is not, then the reader must use the supporting details to determine the main idea.

Read the paragraph. Then look at the chart to see the main idea and supporting details.

It takes many people to build a house. An architect designs the house. Carpenters build the wood frame. A plumber puts in the pipes for water. An electrician puts in the wires for electricity.

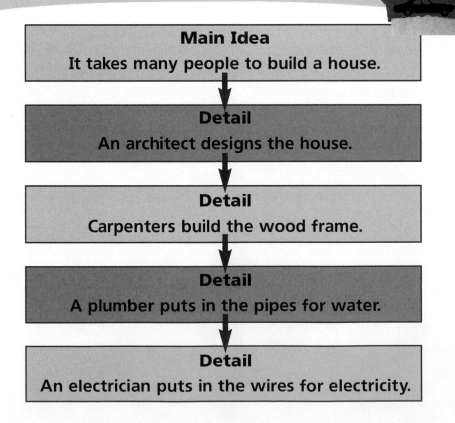

Main Idea
It takes many people to build a house.

Detail
An architect designs the house.

Detail
Carpenters build the wood frame.

Detail
A plumber puts in the pipes for water.

Detail
An electrician puts in the wires for electricity.

Try This

▶ Read the paragraph. Then copy the chart and complete it, using the information in the paragraph.

Many people must work together to make a movie. The actors play the parts. The director tells the actors what to do. A designer plans the costumes. A composer writes the music.

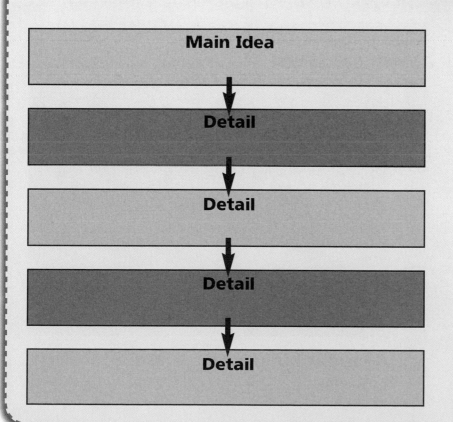

Main Idea

↓

Detail

↓

Detail

↓

Detail

↓

Detail

Vocabulary POWER

Cleaning Up the River ▼

VOCABULARY

project

environment

river

pollution

temperature

crops

permission

success

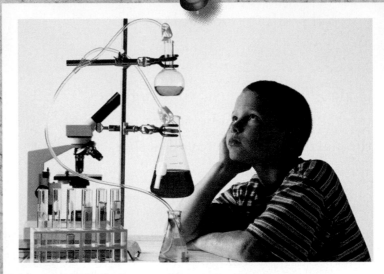

The student worked hard on his science **project**. He is hoping it will be a **success**.

Air **pollution** can make it hard for people to breathe.

A farmer planted these **crops** in the spring.

The student had a question. She asked for **permission** to speak.

It is important to keep the **environment** clean.

In some places the **temperature** can drop quickly in winter. Soon the water in this **river** will freeze.

CLEANING UP THE RIVER

Project: The Environment

Mrs. Noble asked her fifth-grade science class to work together on a project that would help the environment. She asked her students if they could think of any problems with the nearby environment. Two students, Pedro and Jenny, had seen a problem. Pedro said, "There's a layer of slimy green stuff on the Carl River."

The students wanted to find out what the slimy green layer was. Then, they wanted to clean it up!

What was the slimy green stuff on the Carl River?

Pedro and Jenny took some water samples from the Carl River.

Was It Pollution?

The Carl River runs through town near Smith Elementary School. It is a slow-moving river. Last spring, the river turned slimy and green and began to smell bad. Mrs. Noble's class thought the problem might be pollution, but they had to make sure.

The students studied the Carl River for a few months. Each month, they took samples of river water and recorded the temperature of the water. A sample is a small amount of something to study. The students wore thick rubber gloves to protect their hands from the dirty water, and tightly sealed the bottles of water samples. They also wore masks over their mouths and noses because the water smelled bad.

At school the students did many things to find out about the slimy green stuff. They learned about pollution from books and magazines and on the Internet. They tested their samples from the river. Then they organized all their information on a chart.

Some Answers

The class did find signs of pollution in the river. They found that the water contained too much phosphorus. Farmers put phosphorus on their fields because it helps their crops grow. There are many farms near the Carl River. Rain was washing some of the phosphorus from the farms into the river.

The students also found a lot of algae in the water. Algae are tiny living things. The students used a microscope to see the algae. A microscope makes tiny things look bigger.

The students still didn't know what the slimy green stuff was. Pedro learned the answer when he found an article on the Internet about pond scum. Pond scum is a common problem in ponds and in slow-moving rivers like the Carl River. Pond scum is slimy and green, and it smells bad. Pedro thought that the slimy green stuff on the Carl River must be pond scum.

Jenny used a microscope to see a sample of water.

This is the slimy green stuff under a microscope.

80

Pedro and Jenny put in plants to keep phosphorus out of the river.

Plants Save the Day

The students learned that algae need phosphorus to grow. The river had too much phosphorus, so the algae grew very fast. Large numbers of algae grew and died, and it was the dead algae that made the river slimy and green.

Pedro read that plants could stop the phosphorus from washing into the river. The students could plant them near the farms.

The students asked the farmers for permission to put the plants near the farms. The farmers said yes and helped the students. Everyone worked together, and the project was a success.

The next spring, the dead algae were gone, and the river looked and smelled clean again. Mrs. Noble and the students were happy. Their science project really had helped the environment!

Think Critically

1. What was the layer of slimy green stuff on the Carl River?

2. What caused the layer of slimy green stuff?

3. How did Pedro, Jenny, and the other students work with the farmers to help the environment?

4. How could you help the environment in your own community?

Spider Soup ▼

VOCABULARY

house

water

salt

pepper

taste

beans

meal

lesson

We are building a new **house**.

This fountain has very cold **water**.

First, the cook added **salt** to the sauce. Then he added some **pepper** for extra flavor.

I have a music **lesson** every week.

I like to eat **beans**. I like the **taste** of them with butter.

Lunch is my favorite **meal** of the day.

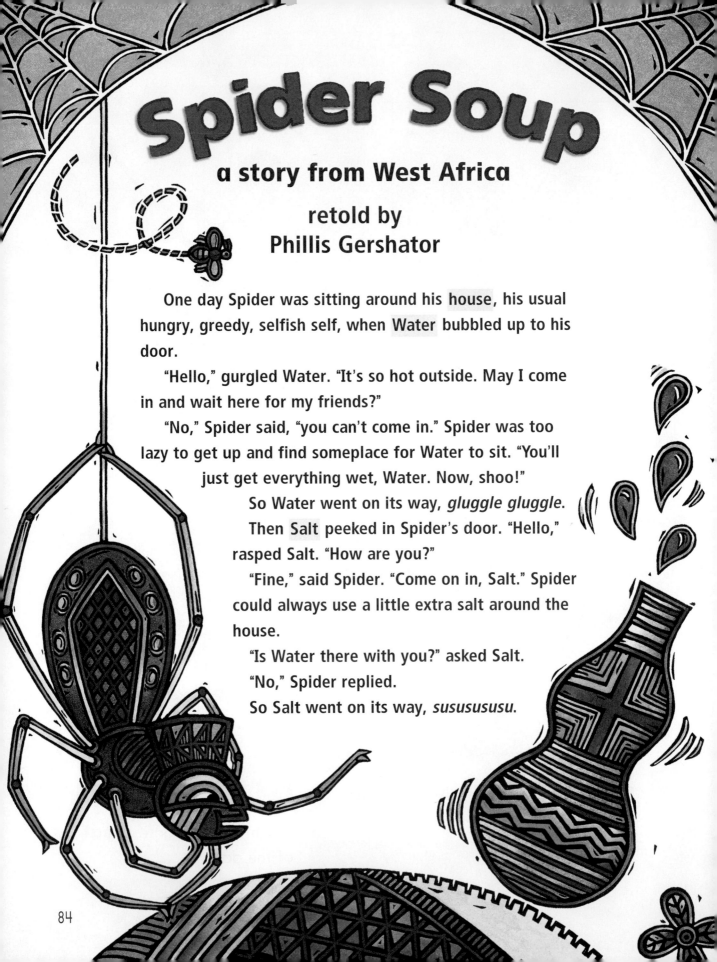

Spider Soup

a story from West Africa

retold by
Phillis Gershator

One day Spider was sitting around his house, his usual hungry, greedy, selfish self, when Water bubbled up to his door.

"Hello," gurgled Water. "It's so hot outside. May I come in and wait here for my friends?"

"No," Spider said, "you can't come in." Spider was too lazy to get up and find someplace for Water to sit. "You'll just get everything wet, Water. Now, shoo!"

So Water went on its way, *gluggle gluggle*.

Then Salt peeked in Spider's door. "Hello," rasped Salt. "How are you?"

"Fine," said Spider. "Come on in, Salt." Spider could always use a little extra salt around the house.

"Is Water there with you?" asked Salt.

"No," Spider replied.

So Salt went on its way, *susususu*.

Then Pepper rolled by. "Hello. How are you?" Pepper rumbled.

"Fine," said Spider. "Stop a minute, why don't you?" Spider liked the taste of pepper on his tongue.

"Is Salt there with you?" asked Pepper.

"No," Spider replied.

So Pepper rolled away, *lululululu.*

Bone was next to pass by, waddling from side to side. "Come in, come in," called Spider. Spider liked the look of Bone. Bone was nice and meaty.

"Is Pepper there with you?" Bone asked.

"No," Spider replied.

So Bone went on its way, *waca waca waca.*

Then Beans skipped up to Spider's house. "Hello. How are you?"

"Fine," said Spider. "Stop and stay awhile, Beans." The thought of Beans made Spider's stomach growl with delight.

"Is Bone there with you?" Beans asked.

"No," Spider replied.

So Beans left in a cloud of dust, *pfff pfff*.

Soon Greens swished along. "Hello, how are you?" Greens politely inquired.

"Fine," said Spider. "Step inside, Greens, and get out of the sun. You wouldn't want to wilt." Greens looked fresh. Spider rubbed his feet together happily when he thought about fresh Greens.

"Is Beans there with you?" Greens asked.

"No," Spider replied.

So Greens continued on its way, *wsh wsh wsh*.

Soup Pot thumped up to Spider's door. "Hello, Spider. I'm supposed to meet Water and all his friends here," Soup Pot said. "We're going to make soup."

Soup Pot looked around Spider's house. "Where's Water?" Soup Pot asked. "We can't make soup without Water."

"Oh," said Spider sadly. "Water's gone."

So Soup Pot left, too, *thumpa thumpa*.

Spider kicked himself eight times, one time with each leg. "If only I had invited Water into my house," he moaned, "I would have ended up with a big soup pot full of soup. Maybe Water or Salt or Pepper or Bone or Beans or Greens alone don't add up to much, but all together, ah! What a meal! Woe is me! Woe is me!"

Who knows if Spider, being Spider, really learned his lesson. But when others heard the story, they understood, and they still say, "When small things come to you, welcome them. Then the larger things will come, too."

Think Critically

❶ Why doesn't Spider let Water into his house?

❷ How does Spider feel after Soup Pot leaves?

❸ What is the lesson of this story?

❹ Do you think Spider learns a lesson? Explain your answer.

Vocabulary POWER

Teams at Work ▼

VOCABULARY

strong

alone

together

teamwork

goal

crew

chores

sharing

When we worked **together**, no one could beat us. **Teamwork** made us champions.

I was **alone** in front of the net. I had to stop the other team from scoring a **goal**.

This man must be **strong** to win the contest.

The members of the **crew** rowed hard.

We were **sharing** the job of carrying the pile of notebooks.

I like to help my mother do **chores** around the house.

TEAMS AT WORK

You are smart and strong enough
to do things on your own.
But when you team with others,
you don't work all alone.
Band members play together—
the cymbals, flute, and horn.
And when a drummer joins them,
a marching band is born!

Teamwork makes things easy—
combining minds is smart!
The job turns out much better
when each person does one part.
There's teamwork in the theater.
Each actor learns one role.
But when the curtain rises,
teamwork is the goal!

You can sail alone with just
the water, wind, and you.
But when you sail with others,
you have a sailing crew!
A crew makes hard work easy.
The ocean can be rough.
A storm is hard to face alone—
a crew is strong enough.

You can play some games alone,
but for most sports you need
a team that plays together,
united to succeed.
Each player has a job to do—
to bat, to catch, to throw.
It's fun to play with others.
Try teamwork, and you'll know!

Everyone has chores to do—
to clean, to paint, to fix.
Sharing makes them easy
in a group of five or six.
The work gets done much faster.
It even can be fun!
Cooperation is the way
to get the big jobs done.

Teamwork makes life easier
than working on your own.
We learn things from each other
and find our skills have grown.
Teamwork takes what's hard in life
and makes it fun and great.
Then, when the job is finished,
the team can celebrate!

MUSICAL INSTRUMENTS

drum

violin

trumpet

flute

triangle

saxophone

Think Critically

1 Give one example of how teamwork makes work easier.

2 What can a player do on a sports team?

3 Would working together make a class project easier and more fun? Why or why not?

4 Is teamwork important in your school? Explain.

Vocabulary POWER

Let the Games Begin! ▼

VOCABULARY

rules

score

sports

athlete

cooperate

leader

competition

win

lose

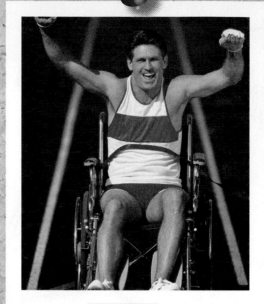

A good **athlete** never stops trying.

I play many **sports**. I know the **rules** of all of them.

96

Always be polite whether you **win** or **lose**.

My friend and I have a friendly **competition** when we play sports.

My brother will **score** many goals this season. He is the **leader** of our team.

Players must **cooperate** by working together.

Let the Games Begin!

by Maya Ajmera and Michael J. Regan

Rules! Who needs them? You do, to play a sport. Rules tell you how to play a game, and what's fair or unfair. In soccer and basketball, the rules tell you how to pass and score points, and what happens when the rules are broken. Rules even tell you what kind of ball to use—after all, the whole game would change if you tried to kick a baseball or dribble a tennis ball.

Track and Field
United States

Ice Hockey
United States vs. Canada

Rules don't work if people ignore them, so most competitive sports have referees, umpires, or judges. These officials take action if someone breaks a rule. In volleyball, if you hit the net while spiking the ball, your team doesn't score the point. In the one-hundred-meter dash, you get disqualified if you leave your own lane. Games are more fun if everyone plays by the rules!

Basketball
Dominican Republic

99

"You shouldn't make fun of the other team if they do badly or if your team wins."
–Rachel, Madagascar

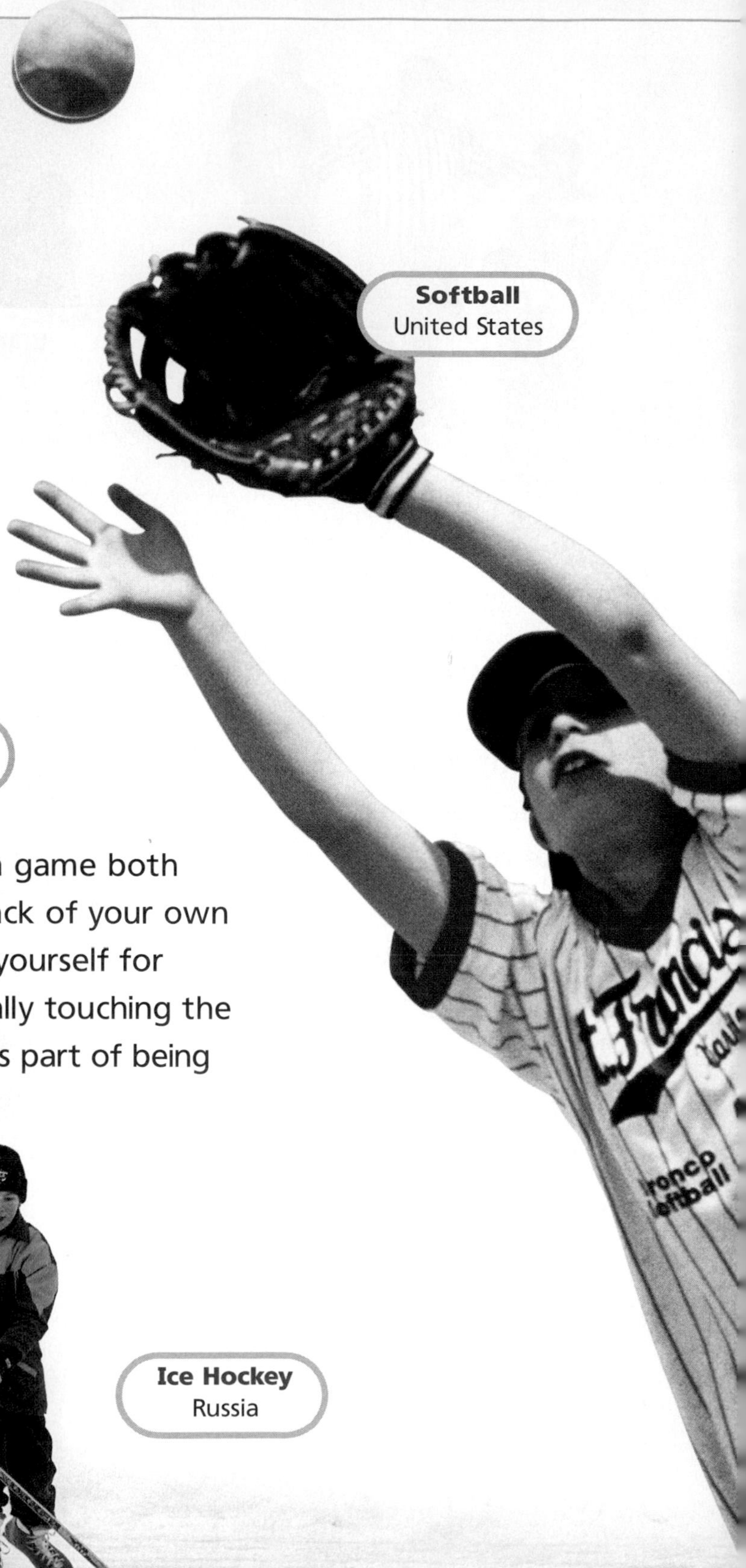

Softball
United States

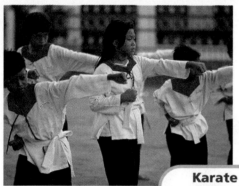

Karate
Indonesia

The way you act helps make a game both fun and fair. In golf, you keep track of your own score. You even call penalties on yourself for breaking a rule, such as accidentally touching the ball before a shot. Being honest is part of being a good sport.

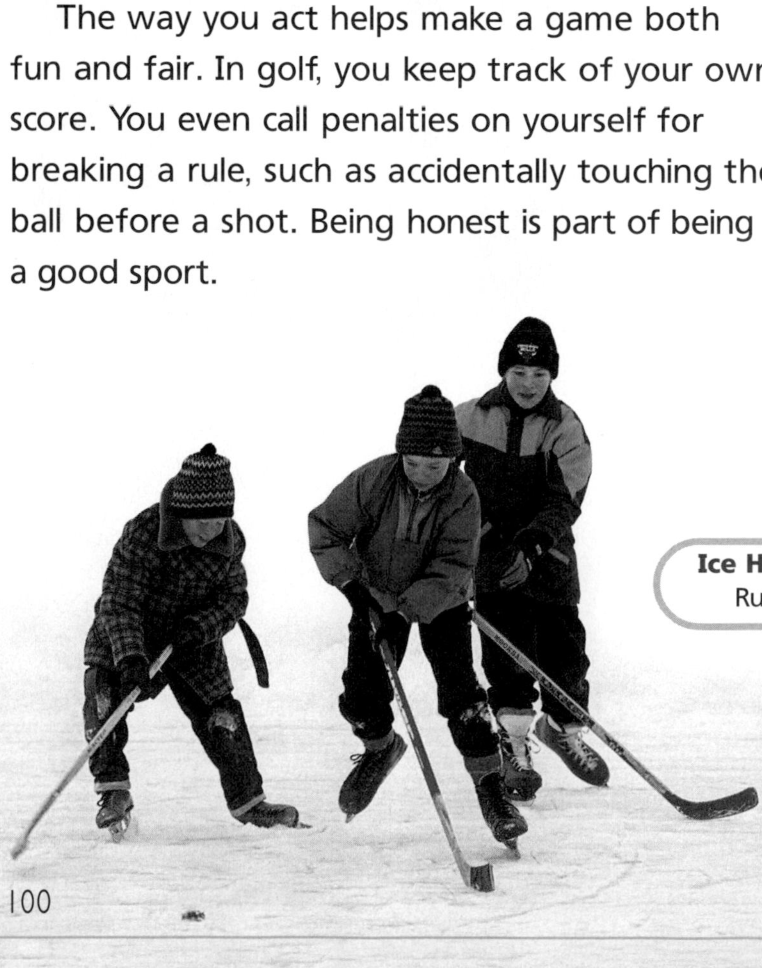

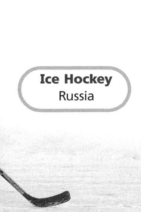

Ice Hockey
Russia

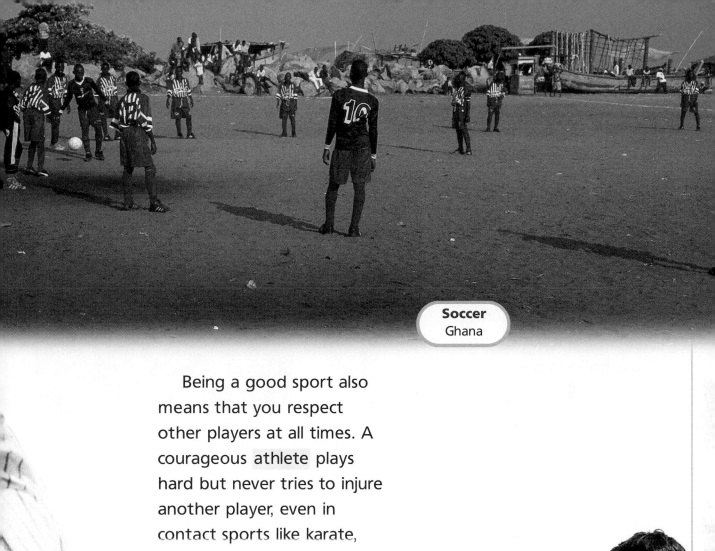

Being a good sport also means that you respect other players at all times. A courageous athlete plays hard but never tries to injure another player, even in contact sports like karate, football, and rugby. Good sportsmanship is global— around the world it's the sign of a champion.

101

To play a team sport you need to cooperate. You might want to drive to the hoop in basketball. Instead, you pass the ball to a player who has an open shot. Helping your team score points is always more important than how good you look.

Basketball
Guatemala

Track and Field
Swaziland

Ice Hockey
Canada

In team sports, players learn to communicate with each other in new ways. With a look or a nod of your head, you can tell a teammate where to pass the hockey puck. You make a sudden move, and before your opponents can react, you are breaking open toward the goal. Good teams create a magic that makes them better than their individual players.

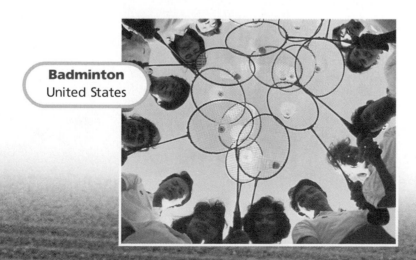

Badminton
United States

Horseback Riding
United States

Soccer
Peru

Everybody can be a leader! Leaders emerge through their skill, attitude, or commitment to the team. The captain of the equestrian team isn't always the best horseback rider. He or she is someone who knows how to motivate the team and how to help teammates through tough situations.

Soccer
Argentina

Different players can be leaders at different times. A goalie can shout guidance across the field or keep the other team from scoring. Players on the sidelines can cheer encouragement as their team heads up and down the field. In sports, there are lots of ways to make a difference.

Softball
United States

Skiing
China

> **"Competition is good because it creates a challenge. Without challenges, life would be boring."**
> **—Hayley, South Africa**

Competition is a big part of sports. To get ready for an event, you and your teammates work harder. Once the contest starts, making a perfect dive, scoring a goal, or winning a race can seem like the most important thing in the world.

Horseback Riding
Mongolia

Track and Field
United Kingdom

During the heat of competition, strong opponents push each other to do better. In a close contest, no one can take it easy. Feeling another runner right on your heels or seeing one just ahead helps you find an extra burst of speed. Successful athletes learn to do their best under pressure.

Judo
United States

> **"Everyone likes to win, and you can if you work hard."**
> *—Sophia, Portugal*

Track and Field
United States

Everybody wants to win. When you do, you feel a rush of excitement. Winning the fifty-meter freestyle makes all your hours of swimming laps worthwhile. When you come from behind or win when you weren't expected to, the victory tastes especially sweet.

Volleyball
Dominican Republic

Basketball
Mongolia

No one likes to lose. If your team fails to block the winning shot in the championship game, you feel upset and maybe even angry. But doing your best is what matters most. Understanding what went wrong will help you the next time. And win or lose, a true champion accepts the outcome gracefully.

Soccer
United States

> "Friendship is important for the team, because if you aren't friends the team won't play well." –*Nicols, Bulgaria*

Soccer
United States

Fans
Japan

Playing sports is a great way to meet new friends. When you support each other on and off the field, you grow to trust and count on each other.

You become better friends by sharing the laughter and celebration of winning and the tears and disappointment of losing. Some of the friendships that develop through sports last a lifetime.

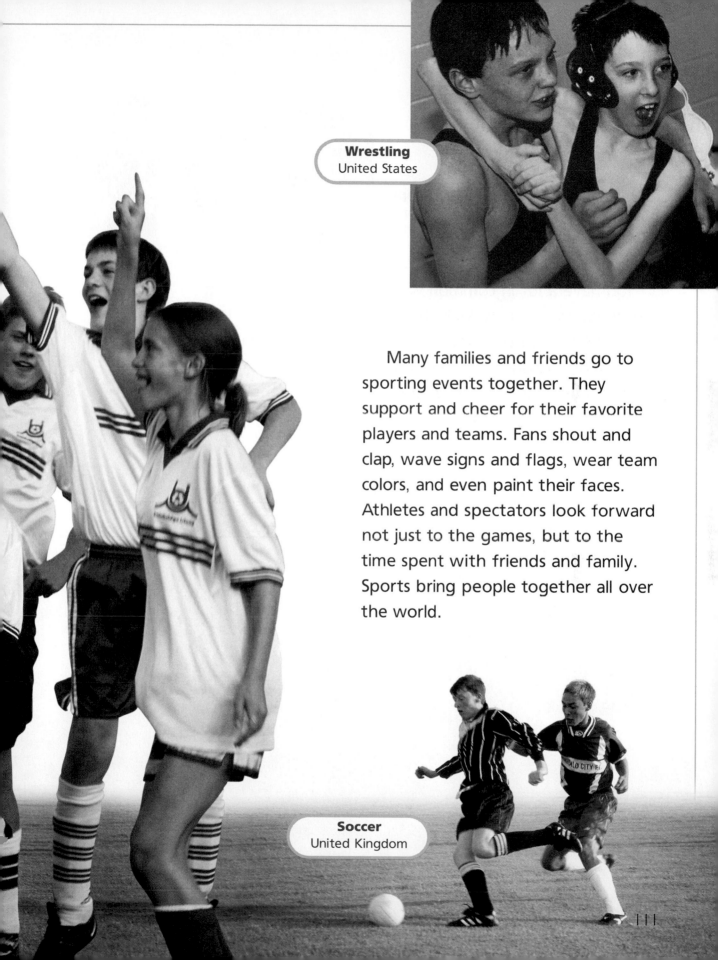

Wrestling
United States

Many families and friends go to sporting events together. They support and cheer for their favorite players and teams. Fans shout and clap, wave signs and flags, wear team colors, and even paint their faces. Athletes and spectators look forward not just to the games, but to the time spent with friends and family. Sports bring people together all over the world.

Soccer
United Kingdom

Ski Jumpers
United States

You have a lot in common with young athletes around the world. Everywhere kids play sports, they practice, learn new skills, and build strong, healthy bodies. They feel joy, excitement, pressure, and the thrill of competition. And no matter where they live or what sport they play, they feel happy when they win and sad when they lose.

Cricket
India

Soccer
Ecuador

Volleyball
Thailand

Some kids like sports for the exercise or the excitement. Some love the challenge of trying to be the best. And some just have fun spending time with their friends. There are lots of reasons to play sports. Pick the one that's right for you, and let the games begin!

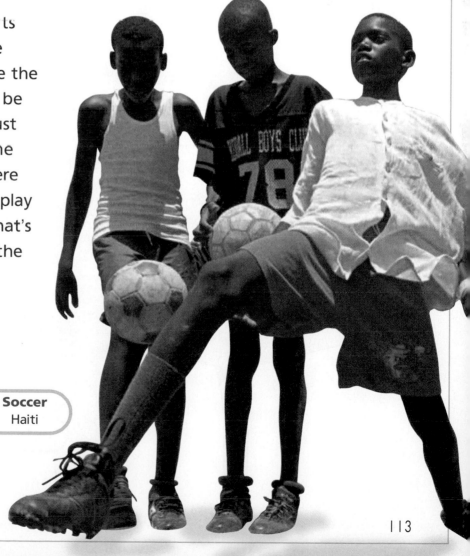

Soccer
Haiti

Sports Equipment

volleyball

volleyball net

backboard

basketball

net

baseball helmet

baseball glove

baseball bat

soccer shoes

soccer ball

Think Critically

1. Why is it important for team members to cooperate when they play sports?

2. Why are rules important in sports?

3. What are some ways to be a leader?

4. How can you show that you are a good team member?

LESSON 10
Unit Review

Review Vocabulary with a Play

STORIES ON STAGE

Bear Builds a House

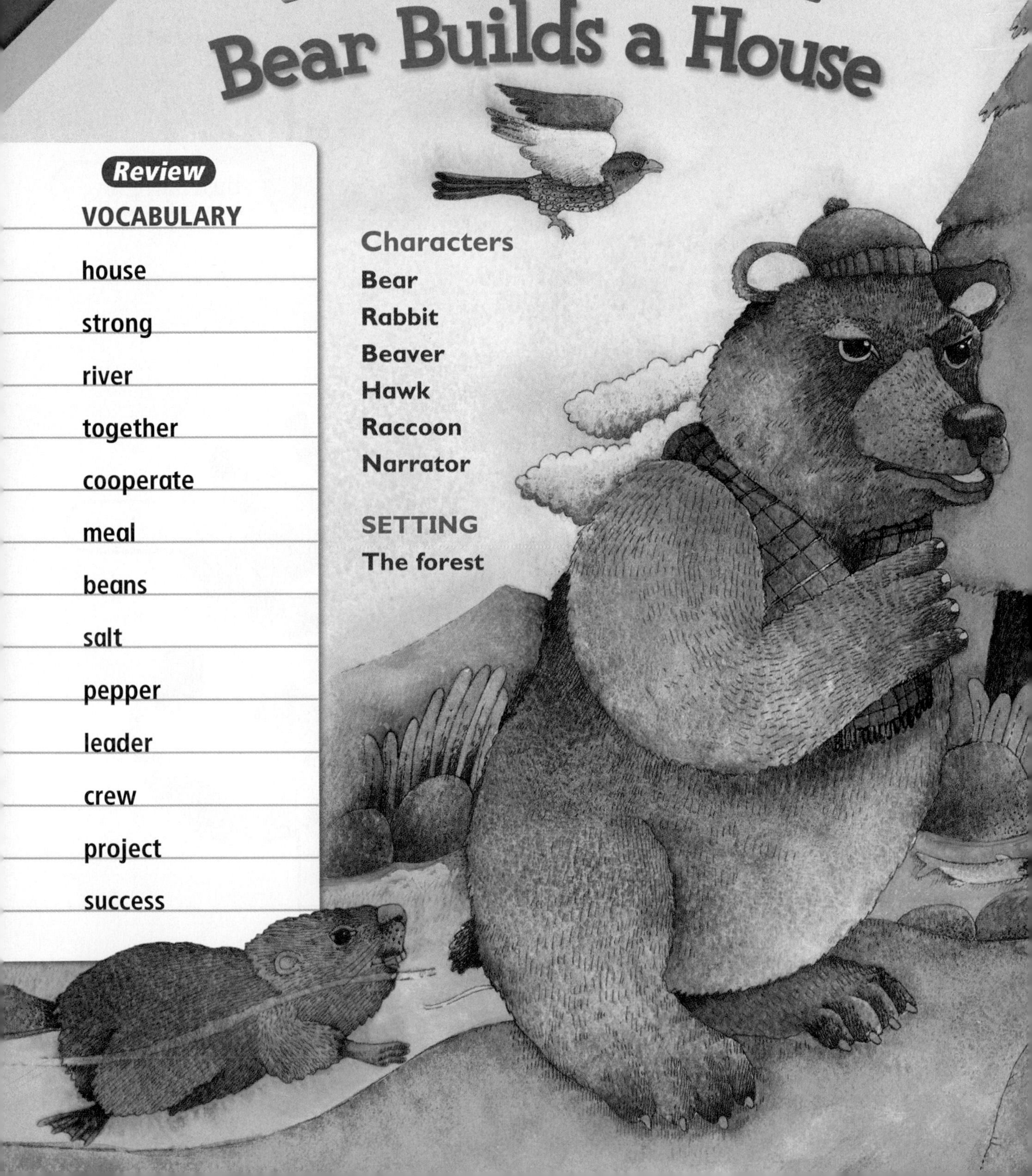

Review
VOCABULARY

- house
- strong
- river
- together
- cooperate
- meal
- beans
- salt
- pepper
- leader
- crew
- project
- success

Characters
Bear
Rabbit
Beaver
Hawk
Raccoon
Narrator

SETTING
The forest

Narrator: It is almost winter in the forest, and Bear is getting worried. He needs to sleep through the winter, but this year he has not found a good place.

Bear: It's beginning to get cold, and winter will be here soon. What shall I do?

Rabbit: Excuse me, Bear. Would you please stop yelling? I'm trying to take a nap.

Bear: Rabbit, how can you nap when winter is coming?

Rabbit: What are you so worried about?

Bear: I still haven't found a place for my winter sleep. Oh, what shall I do?

Rabbit: You could build a house, Bear.

Bear: A house? That's an excellent idea, but I can't
build a house by myself.

Rabbit: I'll help you.

Bear: You are so small, Rabbit. What can you do?

Rabbit: I can pound in nails with my strong back legs.

Bear: Thank you, Rabbit.

Narrator: Beaver is swimming in the river nearby.

Beaver: Excuse me, Bear and Rabbit. I heard you talking.
May I help you build the house?

Bear: How can you help us build a house, Beaver?

Rabbit: Yes, how can you help us?

Beaver: You need wood to build your house. Wood comes
from trees, and I can cut down trees with my sharp teeth.

Bear and Rabbit: Thank you, Beaver! We can all
work together to build a house.

Narrator: Hawk is sitting on a branch nearby.

Hawk: Excuse me, Bear, Rabbit, and Beaver. I heard you talking. I would like to help you, too.

Bear: What can you do, Hawk?

Rabbit: What can a hawk do?

Beaver: Yes, what?

Hawk: Since I can fly, it will be easy for me to put straw on the roof.

Bear, Rabbit, and Beaver: Thank you, Hawk! If we cooperate, we can build a house before winter.

Narrator: Raccoon is playing in some leaves nearby.

Raccoon: Excuse me Bear, Rabbit, Beaver, and Hawk. I heard you talking. I can help you, too.

Bear: There's nothing left for you to do.

Rabbit: Nothing.

Beaver: Nothing at all.

Hawk: Not a thing.

Raccoon: I can bring food. I'll cook you a meal.

Bear, Rabbit, Beaver, and Hawk: Good idea!

Beaver: We need food to give us energy to build the house.

Narrator: Beaver cut down the trees, Rabbit pounded the nails into the wood, and Hawk flew up and covered the roof with straw. Raccoon cooked a fine soup with beans, salt, and pepper. What did Bear do? He was the leader. He made sure the crew worked together.

Bear: Thank you! Now I'll have a place to sleep through the winter.

Narrator: The project was a success. Bear, Rabbit, Beaver, Hawk, and Raccoon became good friends.

Review Activities

Think and Respond

1. How are working together on a science project and being on a sports team alike? How are they different?

2. How did students work together to clean up the river?

3. What do you think Spider will do the next time he has a visitor?

4. Why can working on a team be better than working alone?

5. What do you think would happen if a sports team didn't work together? Why?

LANGUAGE STRUCTURE REVIEW

Talk About Schedules

Work with a partner. Create a short list of questions such as

• What do you usually do in the morning?

• What do you do at noon?

• What do you do at 6:00 in the evening?

Then ask your partner the questions on your list.

Write down your partner's answers. Then make a schedule that shows how your partner spends his or her day.

Omar's Day

6:30 a.m. Wake up.
7:30 a.m. Leave for school.
12:00 p.m. Eat lunch.
3:00 p.m. Go home.
6:00 p.m. Eat dinner.
8:00 p.m. Do homework.
9:00 p.m. Go to bed.

VOCABULARY REVIEW

Be a Vocabulary Detective

Play a game with your classmates, using the Vocabulary Cards. Place the cards face down in a pile. One student picks a card. You and your classmates ask questions to find out which word was picked. Ask questions that your classmate can answer with *yes* or *no*. When you think you know the word, ask, "Is your word_____?" The person who guesses the word picks the next card. The other classmates ask questions again to try to guess the word.

Is your word a noun?

Does your word describe something?

Is your word an action?

Is your word a person?

Is your word something in nature?

Growth, Learning, and Change

We started out small.
Now we're growing up tall,
And we're learning new things every day.
The games that were fun
Years ago in grade one
Are no longer what we want to play.

Growth, learning, and change—
There's so much we can do and explore.
As our school years roll by,
We will change, you and I,
Until we are children no more.

*Sing to the tune of
"Home on the Range."*

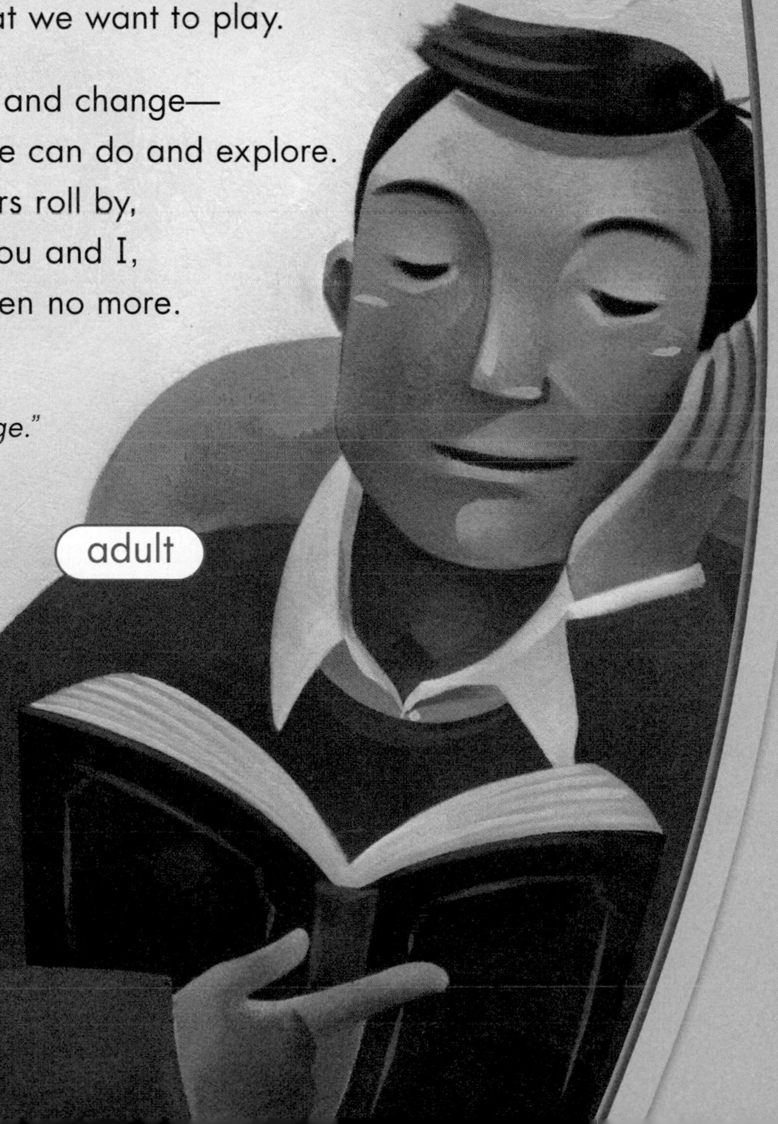

adult

125

Text Structure: Sequence

Authors organize stories and nonfiction selections in different ways. Understanding the **text structure**, or how an author has organized the ideas in a selection, can help you understand what you read.

One way an author may organize a selection is by the **sequence** of events. An author may use signal words, such as *first, next, last, then,* and *finally,* to show the order of events.

Read the paragraph. Then look at the chart to see how the author organized ideas.

Black bears sleep during most of the winter. The bears eat a lot of food in the fall. They find a place to sleep that is protected from the cold weather. Then they sleep through the winter. In the spring, the bears wake up.

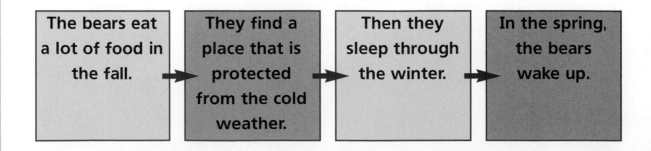

| The bears eat a lot of food in the fall. | They find a place that is protected from the cold weather. | Then they sleep through the winter. | In the spring, the bears wake up. |

Try This

▶ Read the paragraph. Then copy the chart below onto a separate sheet of paper. Use the information in the paragraph to complete the chart.

Butterflies go through four stages of life. An adult butterfly lays an egg. The egg hatches into a caterpillar. The caterpillar spends nearly all of its time eating. Then the caterpillar forms a hard covering around itself. After a few weeks, a butterfly breaks out of the hard covering.

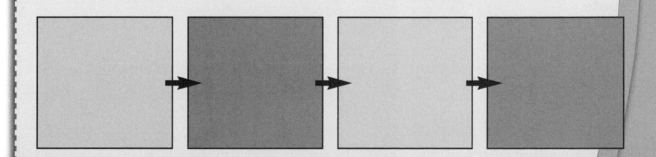

Vocabulary POWER

Nature's Year ▼

VOCABULARY

season

branches

leaves

hatch

roots

oxygen

breathe

cycle

Fall is my favorite **season** of the year. Many **leaves** change color before falling off the tree.

The **branches** of a tree reach toward the sky. The **roots** reach into the ground.

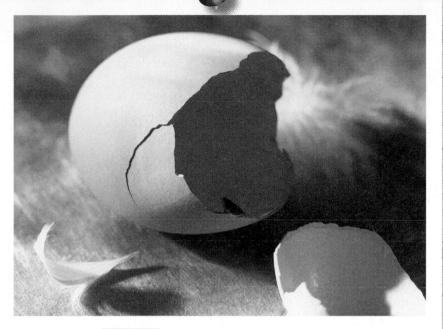

Baby birds **hatch** from eggs.

Oxygen is one of the gases that make up the air. We all need clean air to **breathe**.

Winter and summer are both parts of nature's **cycle**.

Nature's Year

**Some places have four different seasons every year.
As the seasons change, so do some plants and animals.**

Spring

Spring is the season of growth for trees. As the weather gets warmer, tiny buds on the branches open into leaves and flowers. The flowers produce seeds, which can grow into fruits, such as apples or berries. The seeds are blown by the wind or carried by animals to other places. There, new trees will grow. Spring is a time of growth for birds, too. The female bird builds a nest and lays eggs. After the eggs hatch, the female bird and her mate work to find food for the baby birds.

Spring is a time of growth.

Summer

Did you know that green plants are able to make their own food? The way plants, including trees, make food is called photosynthesis. This process occurs mainly in the leaves. In photosynthesis, a tree's leaves use sunlight, carbon dioxide, and water to make food for the tree. Extra food is stored in the roots. This will keep the tree alive through the winter, when there are no leaves to make food.

Photosynthesis not only feeds the tree, it also releases oxygen into the air for animals to breathe.

Trees are important to birds even after their babies have left the nest. They use trees for shade during the day and sleep in their branches at night. They find caterpillars and insects to eat on the tree's leaves and bark.

Birds help trees by eating harmful insects and caterpillars.

Trees create oxygen. Animals, including people, need oxygen to live.

Many North American birds migrate south in the fall.

Fall

As the weather gets colder, trees prepare for winter. They begin growing new buds that will become leaves and flowers next spring. This year's leaves have finished making food. Before they drop off the tree, however, the leaves of many trees turn from green to bright colors—red, orange, and yellow.

The birds prepare for winter, too.

The kinds of insects that they eat will not live through the cold months. This is why birds eat so much in the summer. Some will need their strength to migrate, or fly south, to a warmer place with more food. Many birds migrate thousands of miles each year. A small bird can fly 100 to 250 miles a day during migration.

Many leaves turn bright yellow, orange, and red in the fall.

Winter

The days are short, the nights are long, and the weather is very cold. The trees have lost all their leaves. They look dead, but they are only dormant, or resting. Inside each tree, a liquid called sap moves slowly up from the roots to the rest of the tree. Sap carries the food that keeps the tree alive.

There are small buds on the branches. Each bud holds the tiny beginnings of new leaves and flowers. They will open when spring comes again.

High in the tree's branches, you might see the remains of birds' nests from last spring. The birds that made them may be far away, in a warmer place. In the spring they will return to build new nests. The babies they raised last spring will build their own nests and raise their own babies.

The cycle of life will begin again for both trees and birds.

In winter, the tree is dormant. The birds have migrated south where it is warm and there is more food.

Related Vocabulary

Trees

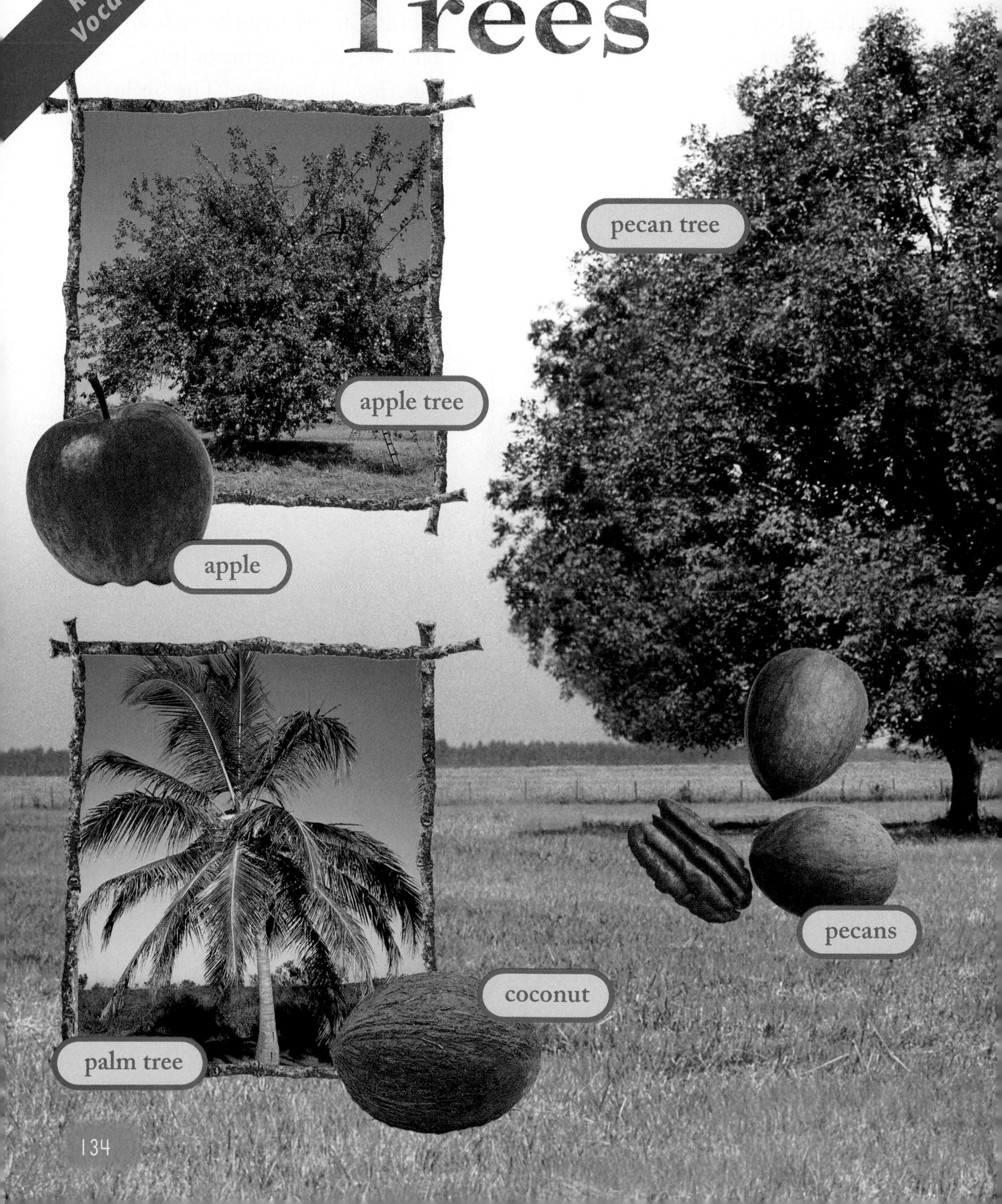

pecan tree
apple tree
apple
pecans
coconut
palm tree

maple tree

maple syrup

olive tree

olives

Think Critically

1. How do trees change through the year?
2. What would happen if birds didn't eat a lot in the summer?
3. Why do trees store sap in their roots?
4. List two interesting facts you learned from this selection.

Vocabulary POWER

Weird Friends ▼

VOCABULARY

predators

protection

survival

enemies

graze

danger

safety

parasites

Animals that kill and eat other animals are **predators**. Animals that live in or on other animals, but do not kill them, are **parasites**.

The lion does not fear **danger**. It has few **enemies**.

Zebras **graze** on the plains of Africa. They stay together for **protection** from predators.

A tortoise can pull its head, tail, and legs inside its shell for **safety**.

A prairie dog can hide under the ground for **survival**.

Weird Friends

Unlikely Allies in the Animal Kingdom

by Jose Aruego and Ariane Dewey

Sometimes in the wild, animals you might think could hurt each other actually help each other in surprising ways. They share food or a home. They warn one another of approaching predators. They cluster side by side for protection. Some animals even give others a good bath. Their survival often depends on these weird friendships.

The Clown Fish and the Sea Anemone

The bright little clown fish needs protection from its enemies. So it chooses a poisonous sea anemone to be its bodyguard. For about an hour, the clown fish carefully darts in and out of the anemone's deadly tentacles. Little by little, it becomes immune to their sting. Then it moves in. The clown fish is safe from predators. So is the anemone, because its enemy, the butterfly fish, is afraid of the clown fish's bite.

The Rhino and the Cattle Egret

As they graze across the plains, a rhino and her calf stir up grasshoppers. But the rhino can't see very well and may not notice danger approaching. So she lets a sharp-eyed cattle egret perch on her back to act as a lookout. The egret is rewarded with an endless feast of grasshoppers.

If the egret spies danger, it screams. And if *that* doesn't get the rhino's attention, it taps on the rhino's head until the mother and baby gallop to safety.

The Forest Mouse and the Beetles

At night, the forest mouse scampers around the rain forest looking for food, with beetles clinging to its fur and face. But the mouse doesn't mind, because the beetles eat the fleas that infest its fur. During the day, while the mouse sleeps, the beetles dismount and eat the bugs in the mouse's burrow. The beetles are always well fed, and the mouse and its house are free of itchy insects.

The Hippo, the Oxpeckers, and the Black Labeo Fish

The hippo can't scrub itself, so it wades into the river and waits for oxpeckers to land on its back. These birds peck off and eat ticks and other bothersome bugs. Meanwhile, in the water below, black labeo fish gobble up anything clinging to the rest of the hippo. When all the parasites have been removed, the hippo naps in the cool mud.

147

The Water Thick-Knees and the Crocodile

A bird called a water thick-knees sometimes builds its nest next to a crocodile's home. When the crocodile leaves to go hunting, the bird watches both of their nests.

If trouble threatens the eggs or young in either nest, the bird screeches until the crocodile comes charging home. The water thick-knees and her family are safe beside their ferocious neighbor, because the crocodile will not eat its baby-sitter.

1 Why do you think the authors chose the title "Weird Friends" for this selection?

2 Why doesn't the rhino attack the cattle egret?

3 How are animal friendships like human friendships?

4 Which animal friendship in this selection interests you the most? Explain why.

Vocabulary POWER

The Way West: One Girl's Story ▼

VOCABULARY

promised

prepare

wagon

supper

railroad

prairie

barrel

farmer

A wild horse runs on the **prairie**.

Many people traveled west by covered **wagon**. The government **promised** them good, inexpensive farmland there.

The **railroad** opened up great sections of the United States. This helped **prepare** the way for people to move west.

A **farmer** may grow many kinds of foods. Some he will sell, but some he will keep for his family's **supper**.

A large **barrel** can hold enough drinking water for a week or more.

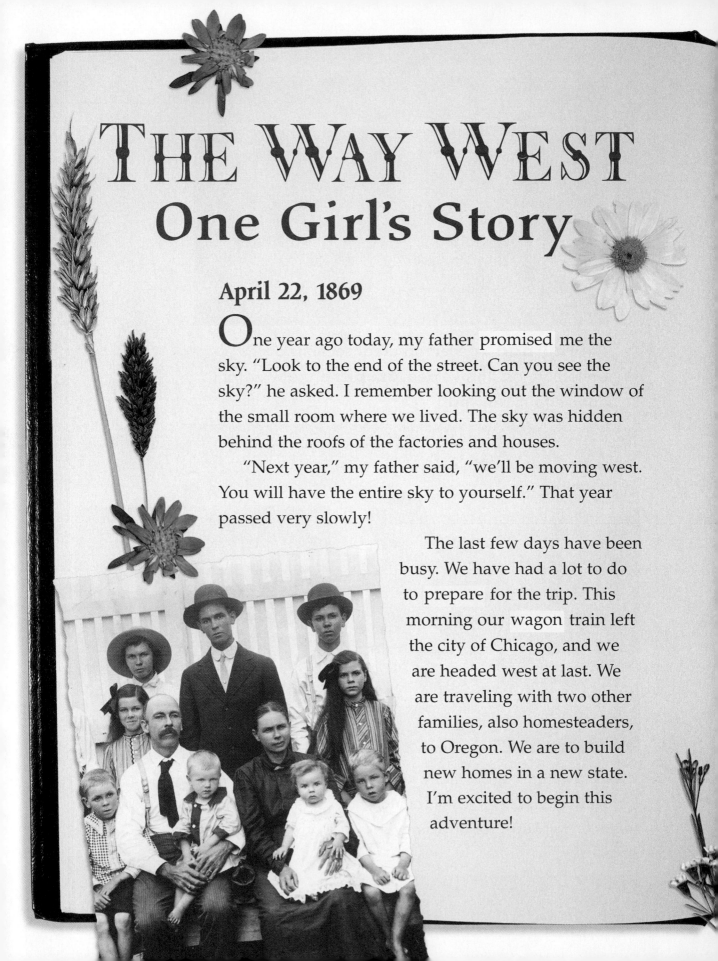

THE WAY WEST
One Girl's Story

April 22, 1869

One year ago today, my father promised me the sky. "Look to the end of the street. Can you see the sky?" he asked. I remember looking out the window of the small room where we lived. The sky was hidden behind the roofs of the factories and houses.

"Next year," my father said, "we'll be moving west. You will have the entire sky to yourself." That year passed very slowly!

The last few days have been busy. We have had a lot to do to prepare for the trip. This morning our wagon train left the city of Chicago, and we are headed west at last. We are traveling with two other families, also homesteaders, to Oregon. We are to build new homes in a new state. I'm excited to begin this adventure!

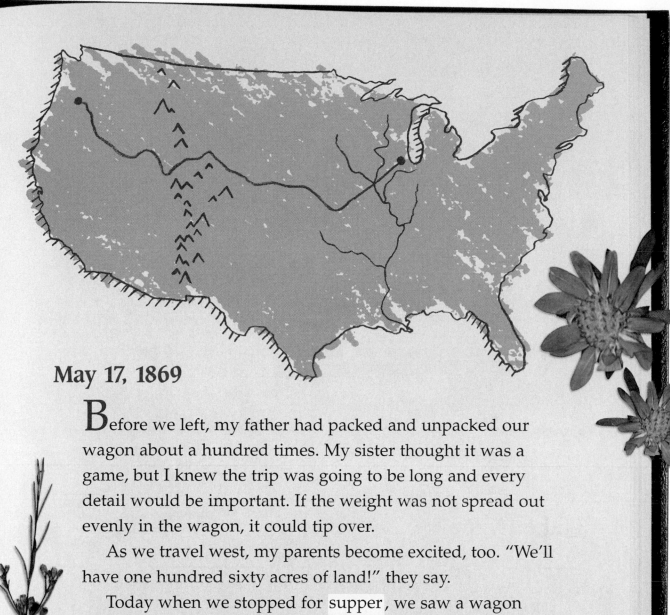

May 17, 1869

Before we left, my father had packed and unpacked our wagon about a hundred times. My sister thought it was a game, but I knew the trip was going to be long and every detail would be important. If the weight was not spread out evenly in the wagon, it could tip over.

As we travel west, my parents become excited, too. "We'll have one hundred sixty acres of land!" they say.

Today when we stopped for supper, we saw a wagon traveling east. A man was in the wagon alone, and like good neighbors, we invited him to eat with us. After supper he told us about his journey west in 1849 to look for gold. Like most people, he didn't find any gold, but he stayed in California and opened his own supply store. Now he was heading back east to live with his brother.

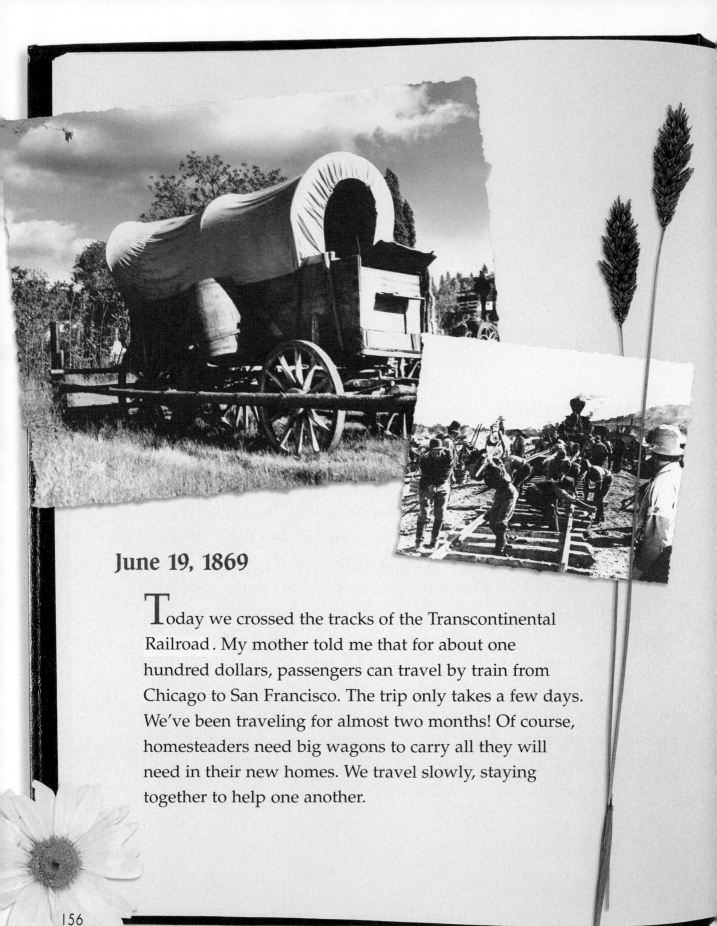

June 19, 1869

Today we crossed the tracks of the Transcontinental Railroad. My mother told me that for about one hundred dollars, passengers can travel by train from Chicago to San Francisco. The trip only takes a few days. We've been traveling for almost two months! Of course, homesteaders need big wagons to carry all they will need in their new homes. We travel slowly, staying together to help one another.

July 12, 1869

The prairie seems endless. The land is flat, and there are no trees. As far as the eye can see, there is only grass. In the summer, if it hasn't rained for a long time, the grass dries up and the prairie can easily catch fire. We are always careful to completely put out the fires we use for cooking.

August 8, 1869

It's very hot, and the land is dry. It's hard to find water. The days are usually boring, but today something exciting happened! First, we heard a strange noise from far away. "It's a cattle drive!" someone shouted. Soon we saw a huge group of moving cattle. My father explained to me that the cattle are taken to a town where there is a railroad station. From there, trains take the cattle to cities such as Chicago. "Do the cows have to pay one hundred dollars for the trip, too?" I joked. Everybody laughed.

September 5, 1869

This afternoon we stopped at a trading post, a place where travelers can get food and other supplies. The trader let us fill our water barrel from the well behind his house.

His house was made of sod, or soil held together by grass. His wife told us it was hard to keep clean. "It's always full of dust, and sometimes snakes slip in, too!" she said.

I decided to wait outside.

September 23, 1869

Today we arrived at a farm. The farmer is a good friend of my uncle. We were glad to hear from him that my uncle is waiting for us. My uncle came here last year to set up his own homestead, and he will be our neighbor. The farmer told us stories about life on the frontier. He said that at one time millions of grasshoppers came—so many that they covered the sky like a dark cloud. I wonder what kinds of stories we'll be telling this time next year!

September 25, 1869

Today, after more than five months of traveling, we arrived at my uncle's farm. We couldn't believe what we saw! His house is made of wood, not sod. All around it are fields of wheat. My uncle explained to us that it is a kind of wheat that needs less water to grow. He also showed us a special kind of steel plow that he uses to turn over the hard soil.

Tonight, for the first time in months, I slept under a roof. The truth is, I couldn't sleep. I got up quietly and left the house. Outside I found my parents standing under the starry sky.

When my father saw me, he smiled and pointed up. "Now you have the sky all to yourself," he said. The promise had come true.

Inside the COVERED WAGON

photo album

lantern

cup

spoon

knife

plate

fork

dry goods

bacon

chair

Think Critically

1 What kinds of problems did the homesteaders face while traveling west?

2 Why did people move west?

3 What might have happened if the homesteaders didn't travel in groups?

4 Would you have liked to travel west with the homesteaders? Why or why not?

Vocabulary POWER

Someplace Else ▼

VOCABULARY

orchard

leaving

visit

highway

apartment

seashore

forest

desert

Many apples grow in this **orchard**.

My grandparents have an **apartment** in the city. I like to **visit** them there.

This **highway** crosses ten states. We are **leaving** on a long car trip today.

Some families enjoy spending time together at the **seashore**.

Thousands of trees grow in this **forest**.

A **desert** is a place where little rain falls.

Someplace Else

by Carol P. Saul • illustrated by Barry Root

All her life Mrs. Tillby had lived in the white house by the apple orchard. All her life Mrs. Tillby had tended the trees and picked and sold apples. All her life Mrs. Tillby wondered how it would be to live someplace else.

One morning Mrs. Tillby woke up and went downstairs. Her son Wes was fixing breakfast.

"Wes," said Mrs. Tillby. "All my life I've lived in this house, watching the orchard change with the seasons. All my life I've wondered how it would be to live someplace else, and now is the time for me to try. So tomorrow I'm leaving to visit your brother Les in the big city. If it suits me, I'll stay."

"But . . . Mother!" said Wes. "This house has always been your home. Where else would you want to live?"

"I don't know, dear," said Mrs. Tillby. "I just know that I want to try living someplace else."

The next day Mrs. Tillby put her suitcase in the back of the old green truck. She hugged Wes good-bye. Then Mrs. Tillby drove off down the road.

The country road that wound around the apple orchard became a six-lane highway. Cars and trucks rushed by. Houses gave way to tall buildings.

Mrs. Tillby pulled up in front of Les's apartment house. It was forty stories high. Les was waiting for her, looking handsome in his gray banker's suit.

"Welcome to the city, Mother!" said Les, kissing her on the top of her head. "I know you're going to love it here!"

"Thank you, dear," said Mrs. Tillby. She stood on tiptoe to reach his cheek. "It looks that way to me!"

Mrs. Tillby was happy in the city. She went to museums and theaters and stores and restaurants. She saw all sorts of people and tried all kinds of food. At night, from her bedroom window, she could see the lights of the city shining brighter than the stars.

But after a few weeks she wanted to move on.

"I can see why you love city life, Les," said Mrs. Tillby, "with all the hustle and bustle, and so much to see and do. But it doesn't feel like home to me, so I want to try living someplace else."

"Oh, Mother," said Les, "stay a while longer. You haven't seen half of the city."

Mrs. Tillby patted Les's hand.

"You're a dear boy," she said, "and a lovely host. But tomorrow I'm leaving to visit your sister Tess at the seashore. If it suits me, I'll stay."

The next day Mrs. Tillby put her suitcase in the back of the old green truck. She hugged Les good-bye and set off toward the highway.

Soon the six-lane highway thinned out. The tall buildings gave way to houses again. Seagulls swooped and called overhead. Mrs. Tillby smelled salt in the air.

Mrs. Tillby pulled up to Tess's house. It stood on stilts at

the edge of the ocean. Tess was waiting for her, wearing a fisherman's yellow slicker. The twins were waiting, too.

"Grandma! Grandma!" they cried.

"Welcome to the seashore, Mother!" said Tess. "You'll just love it here!"

"Thank you, dear," said Mrs. Tillby, hugging everyone at once. "I'm sure I will."

Mrs. Tillby did like the house on stilts. From her window she could see far out over the ocean. She spent hours gathering shells with the twins and helped Tess cook fresh fish and chowder for dinner. Every evening Mrs. Tillby went for a barefoot walk along the shore. At night the sound of the waves lulled her to sleep.

But after a few weeks she needed to move on.

"I understand why you love living by the shore, Tess," said Mrs. Tillby. "The sea is always changing, and the air is ever so clear. But it doesn't feel like home to me, so I want to try living someplace else."

"Oh, Mother," said Tess, "you haven't been here long enough. Wait until you see the wild waves at neap tide!"

Mrs. Tillby patted her hand.

"You're a dear girl," she said, "and you've made me very welcome. But tomorrow I'm leaving to visit your brother Jackson in the mountains. If it suits me, I'll stay."

The next day Mrs. Tillby hugged Tess and the twins. She put her suitcase in the back of the old green truck and drove off down the road.

The road narrowed and became twisty. Sand dunes gave way to hills, and hills to mountains. Hawks wheeled above her.

Mrs. Tillby pulled up to Jackson's house. It was made of stone and sat on the edge of a cliff.

Jackson came out to greet her in his thick woolen lumberjacket. He wrapped his mother in a big bear hug.

"Welcome to the mountains, Mother!" he said. "You're going to love it here!"

"Thank you, dear," said Mrs. Tillby, adjusting her glasses. "I can't imagine anything nicer."

Mrs. Tillby loved the mountains and the smell of pine that filled the air. Every night she lit a fire in the great stone fireplace. Winter came, and snow fell like a thick white blanket. Jackson's wife taught her how to ski.

But after a few weeks she felt like moving on.

"I know why you love the mountains, Jackson," said Mrs. Tillby. "You can see for miles around, and there is more wildlife than I ever dreamed of. But it just doesn't feel like home to me. I'm going to try someplace else."

"Oh, Mother," said Jackson, "at least stay the winter. And you must see the mountains in early spring."

Mrs. Tillby patted his hand.

"You're a dear boy," she said, "and you've treated me like a guest. But I am leaving tomorrow."

"But Mother Tillby," said Jackson's wife, whose name was Bess. "Where will you go? You're tired of the orchard, you've tried the mountains and the seashore, and big-city life doesn't suit you. What is left?"

"I don't know, dear," said Mrs. Tillby. "There must be someplace else."

The next day Mrs. Tillby put her suitcase in the back of the old green truck. She hugged Jackson and his wife, and drove down the mountain road.

Mrs. Tillby tried living in lots of places. She stayed in a cabin by a lake and in a fire tower high above a forest. She stayed in an adobe hut in the middle of the desert. She even spent time on a riverboat!

But everywhere she went, it was the same. Mrs. Tillby was always happy at first. After a few weeks she always wanted to move on.

One morning Mrs. Tillby put her suitcase in the back of the old green truck for the last time. Wearily she set off back toward the apple orchard.

"All my life," said Mrs. Tillby as she drove, "I've wanted to live someplace else. Now I've tried all kinds of places, and nothing suits me."

Mrs. Tillby had almost reached the road that led to the orchard when she came to a crossroads. There, parked at a gas station, she saw a shiny silver trailer. FOR SALE read the sign in the window. Mrs. Tillby leaped out of the old green truck. She asked to see the inside of the trailer.

The silver trailer had a cozy bedroom, a tiny bathroom, and a kitchen that folded out of sight.

Mrs. Tillby bought it on the spot.

Now, every few weeks, Mrs. Tillby sets off in the old green truck with the shiny silver trailer attached behind. Sometimes she visits Les in the city, or Tess at the seashore, or Jackson and his wife in the mountains.

Sometimes she stays in other places. And in the autumn Mrs. Tillby goes back to the white house by the orchard to help Wes pick and sell apples.

Mrs. Tillby is always home, and she is always someplace else.

Think Critically

1. Why does Mrs. Tillby think about living someplace else?

2. What do you learn about Mrs. Tillby from reading the story?

3. How is Mrs. Tillby "always home" and "always someplace else"?

4. In which of the places Mrs. Tillby visits would you most like to live? Why?

LESSON 15
Unit Review

Review Vocabulary with a Play

STORIES ON STAGE

What Kind of Fish Is This?

Review VOCABULARY

- forest
- visit
- prepared
- safety
- protection
- promised
- cycle
- hatch

Characters

Narrator
Yoko
Mark
Tomás
Rita
Mr. Kinsley

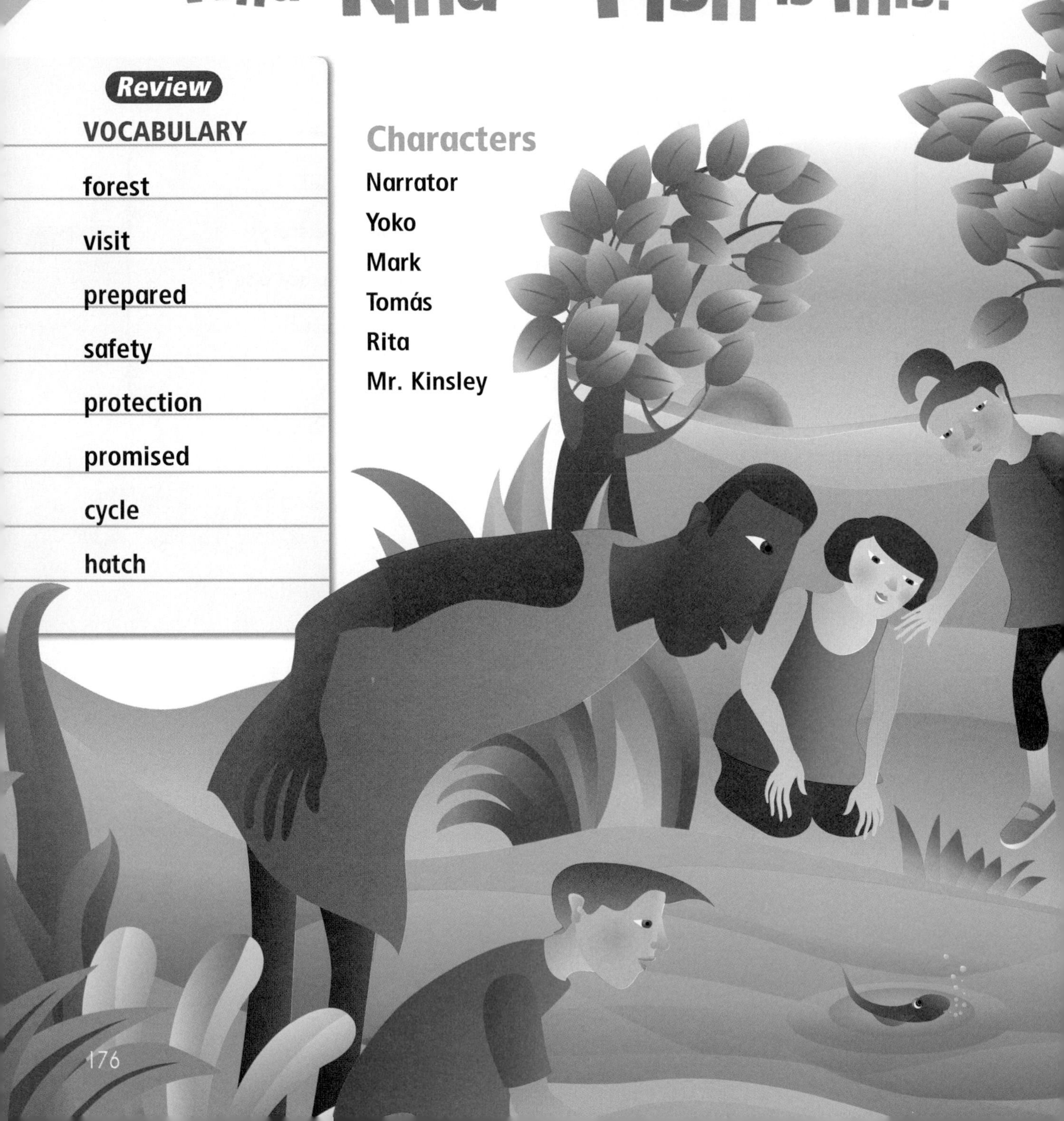

Scene 1

SETTING: A pond at a neighborhood park near a forest

Narrator: Yoko, Tomás, Rita, and Mark are on a class field trip to visit a pond. Tomás sees something in the water.

Tomás: What's that?

Rita: It's a tiny fish!

Yoko: What kind of fish is it?

Mark: I don't know.

Yoko: It has a small tail, but it swims fast.

Mark: It has a big head!

Tomás: Can we take it back to school, Mr. Kinsley? We can do some research to find out what kind of fish it is.

Mr. Kinsley: Yes, we can put it in this jar.

Mark: Be careful not to hurt it.

Narrator: Mr. Kinsley dips a jar into the pond and takes the fish.

Rita: It can be a class pet!

All: Great idea!

Scene 2

Narrator: The fish is in a fish bowl. Mr. Kinsley is talking to the class.

Mr. Kinsley: Remember, students, a pet is a responsibility. You have to be prepared to take care of it. A pet needs its owner to give it safety and protection.

Tomás: What kind of fish is it, Mr. Kinsley?

Mr. Kinsley: That's what I want *you* to find out.

Yoko: Should we give it a name?

Mark: How about Fins?

Rita: Okay, but wait! This fish doesn't have any fins!

Mr. Kinsley: That's right, Rita. I want all of you to observe Fins for a few weeks. See if you can find out exactly what he is.

Tomás: I guess we should call him Finless.

All: Yes! Let's call him Finless.

Scene 3

SETTING: In the classroom, after school

Narrator: Two weeks have passed. Yoko, Tomás, Rita, and Mark spend time each day researching their mystery fish.

Yoko: Finless looks a little like the catfish in this book.

Tomás *(taking the book)*: Let's see. No, Finless is too small.

Rita: What do we know about Finless?

Mark: Well, he's got a long tail.

Tomás: He never ate the fish food we gave him.

Yoko: True. Mr. Kinsley put these plants in the bowl. He said Finless eats the algae off the plants.

Tomás: Finless isn't like any fish we've read about in books or on the Internet.

Rita: Mr. Kinsley promised we would find out what Finless is. He said we have to be patient.

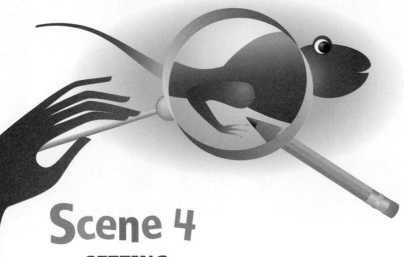

Scene 4

SETTING: In the classroom, Monday morning

Narrator: A few more weeks have passed.

Yoko *(looking at Finless with a magnifying glass)*: Look at this! I see something strange about Finless.

Tomás *(taking the magnifying glass)*: Let me see. What are those things near his tail? They look like little legs.

Mark: Legs? Fish don't have legs!

Mr. Kinsley: This is why I said to be patient.

Rita: Finless never had legs before, Mr. Kinsley.

Mr. Kinsley: That's because he grew them, Rita. The back legs grow first. Two front legs will grow soon now.

Tomás: Wait a minute. If fish don't have legs, then…

Yoko: …Finless isn't a fish at all, is he?

Mr. Kinsley: No, he isn't, Yoko. He's a tadpole.

Rita: What's a tadpole, and why is it growing legs?

Mr. Kinsley: A tadpole is a young frog.

All the Students: A frog?

Mr. Kinsley: Yes. A frog's life cycle begins when a female frog lays eggs. Then tadpoles hatch from the eggs. Finless won't be a tadpole much longer. His legs will get bigger, and his tail will get smaller. Soon Finless will be a frog.

Rita: That's *amazing!*

Yoko: So that's why we couldn't find information about him in the fish books!

Tomás: Now that we know what Finless is, we should start learning about frogs.

Narrator: By the time Finless grew into a frog, the students had learned a lot. They knew they should return him to his home. They took Finless back to the pond, said good-bye, and let him go.

Review Activities

Think and Respond

1. Compare two types of changes that you read about in this unit.

2. Why do birds migrate?

3. Describe the relationship between two of the animals in "Weird Friends." How would their lives change if they were not friends?

4. How did the railroad help the United States grow?

5. Why does Mrs. Tillby travel all around the country in the story "Someplace Else"?

LANGUAGE STRUCTURE REVIEW

Follow and Give Directions

Work with your classmates. Write down directions for drawing a simple picture, such as

- Draw a square.
- Draw a triangle in the square.
- Draw a smaller triangle to the left of the square.
- Draw a circle above the square.

Read aloud these directions to your classmates. They will try to draw the picture by following your directions. Then switch roles.

Spin for a Sentence

Form two groups. You will need a set of Vocabulary Cards and the spinner from *Game Board 2*. Divide the cards between the two groups. Pick a card and then use the spinner.

- If you spin a 1, you use the word in a sentence.
- If you spin a 2, the person to your left uses the word in a sentence.
- If you spin a 3, the person to your right uses the word in a sentence.

Take turns playing until you have used all the Vocabulary Cards. You can use your glossary if you need help remembering what a word means.

gallery

painting

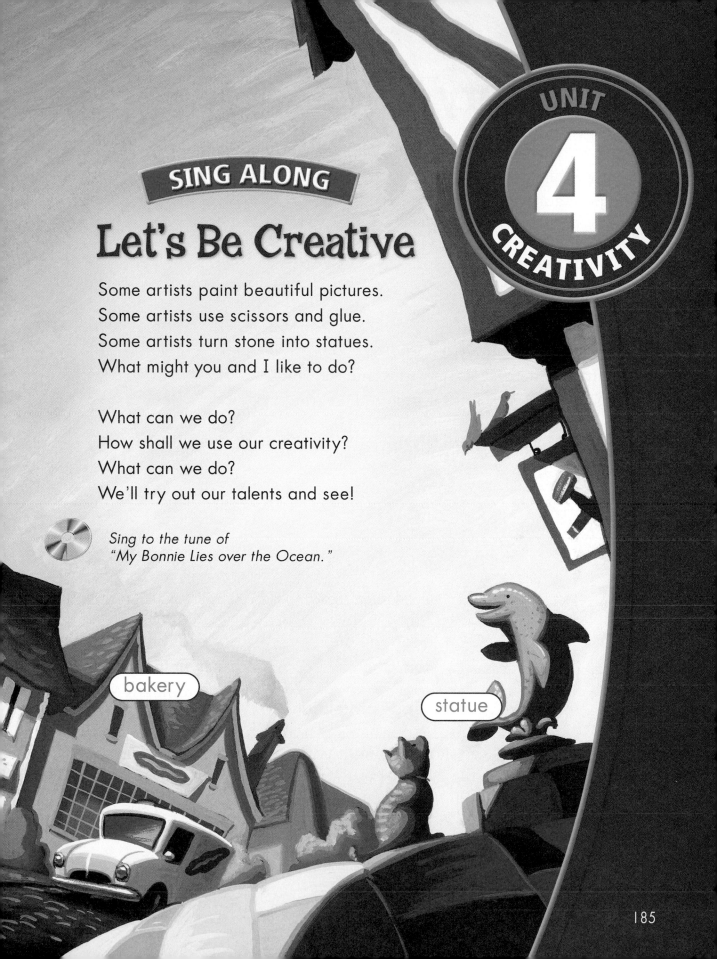

SING ALONG

Let's Be Creative

Some artists paint beautiful pictures.
Some artists use scissors and glue.
Some artists turn stone into statues.
What might you and I like to do?

What can we do?
How shall we use our creativity?
What can we do?
We'll try out our talents and see!

*Sing to the tune of
"My Bonnie Lies over the Ocean."*

bakery

statue

Vocabulary in Context

Some words have more than one meaning. To figure out the correct meaning, use the **context** of the word. This means looking at nearby words and sentences.

Read the paragraph. Then look at the chart to identify the meaning of the underlined words.

One popular <u>kind</u> of art is pottery. To make a piece of pottery, an artist starts with some clay and mixes it with water until it is soft. Then the artist begins to <u>form</u> the clay into shapes such as cups, bowls, and dishes.

Multiple-Meaning Word	Meanings	Context Clues
kind	1. one type of something 2. gentle or helpful	The words *art* and *pottery* help show that *kind* means "one type of something."
form	1. a document with blanks to be filled in 2. to make into a shape	The word *shapes* tells the reader that *form* is something the artist does to the clay.

Try This

▶ Read the paragraph below. Then, on a separate sheet of paper, copy the chart. Complete the chart by using the context clues to find the correct meaning of the word.

Every year our class puts on a play. This year María has the lead role. The director says María has to <u>project</u> her voice so the audience can hear her. We invite all of our family and friends to <u>watch</u> us perform. My job is to <u>record</u> the performance so we can listen to it later.

Multiple-Meaning Word	Meanings	Context Clues
project	1.	
	2.	
watch	1.	
	2.	
record	1.	
	2.	

Vocabulary POWER

Pueblo Storyteller ▼

VOCABULARY

crafts

traditions

generation

language

figures

fireplace

pottery

broken

A **language** may be written or spoken.

Wood carving is one of many **crafts** that are popular in the United States.

188

The fire in the **fireplace** kept the room warm.

My grandfather's costume is one of many **traditions** that have been passed down from his **generation** to mine.

This artist makes **pottery**. She knows that, when dry, clay pots are easily **broken**.

My uncle made these clay **figures**.

Pueblo
Storyteller

by Diane Hoyt-Goldsmith
photographs by Lawrence Migdale

April lives with her grandparents in the Cochiti Pueblo near Santa Fe, New Mexico. Although many Cochiti people work or go to school outside the pueblo, they still follow the ways of their ancestors in their crafts and celebrations. The older family members pass these traditions on to the younger generation, just as they have for years.

important person in our culture. This is also why so many potters in the Cochiti Pueblo make clay figures of the storyteller.

When my grandmother makes a Storyteller, she always thinks about her own grandfather. When she was a young girl, she enjoyed many happy hours in his company. In those days, they didn't have a television or a gas heater. She would sit on her grandfather's lap near a little fireplace in the corner of the room and listen to him tell stories about his life.

Working on the clay figure, my grandmother creates a face that looks like her grandfather's. She gives him the traditional hairstyle of a pueblo man from the old days. She models the clay to show his long hair pulled back in a loop behind his head with a colorful band to hold it in place.

My grandmother makes arms and legs from smaller cylinders. She

April's grandfather kneads the fine sand into the clay indoors, where the wind will not blow it away.

Since the early days of pueblo life, our people have learned about the past by listening to storytellers. Until now, we have never had a written language, so many of our stories cannot be found in books. This is why the storyteller is such an

attaches these to the body with bits of moistened clay. Then she models boots or moccasins from the clay.

She always makes his face look very kind. He sits with his mouth open, as if he were singing a song or telling a story. His eyes are closed as he thinks in the backward way, remembering the past.

Each potter who makes a Storyteller figure works in a different style. Some Storytellers are large and some are small. Many potters create the figure of a woman, remembering a favorite aunt or grandmother. Others, like my grandmother, design a figure that reminds them of their grandfather.

 April's grandmother shows her how to join the edges of the slab with a little water to form a cylinder.

🏠 *A Storyteller is left to dry in the corner of the kitchen. On the shelf above the clay figure, you can see a ladle made from a gourd.*

When the Storyteller is complete, my grandmother makes many tiny figures out of the clay. These are shaped like little pueblo children and she attaches them, one by one, to the Storyteller figure. She crowds them all onto his lap, so they can listen carefully to his tales, just as she did so long ago.

My grandmother adds as many children as she can fit. She tells me that on every Storyteller she makes, there is one child who looks just like me! This makes me feel very special.

After all the modeling is finished, the pottery is left to dry. This takes many days.

When the pottery is hard and dry, it is my grandfather's turn to work on it. He rubs the surfaces of the pottery with sandpaper until they are smooth enough to paint. My grandfather tells me he likes to be in a happy, patient mood when he is sanding the pottery. The work must be done carefully. It cannot be rushed.

Sometimes the pottery will break or crack before it is finished. Instead of throwing the ruined pottery away in the garbage, the pueblo potters give the clay back to the earth where it came from. My grandfather often takes a broken pot down to the river and throws it in the water. Sometimes he will take the broken pieces back up into the hills near the pueblo.

 *April's grandmother makes the figure of a little child. Then she attaches the child to the body of the Storyteller with bits of moistened clay.*

After the pieces are sanded, my grandmother covers them with a thin layer of white clay that has been mixed with water, called slip. When the slip dries, it gives the pottery a clean, white surface that can be polished and painted.

To get a shiny surface, my grandmother polishes her pots with special stones. These polishing stones are very important to the pueblo potters. Each one gives a different patina or shine. Polishing stones are treasured, and the good ones are passed down from one generation to the next.

My grandmother likes to paint her pottery in a very quiet place. She needs to concentrate so that the lines she draws will be straight and the shapes that she makes will be beautiful.

For the red color, my grandmother uses a clay that is mixed with water. For the black, she uses guaco (GWA-koh), an inky liquid made by boiling down a wild plant that grows in the fields near our house. It is called Rocky Mountain beeweed. This same plant is something we pick in the spring and eat as one of our vegetables.

After my grandmother finishes painting the pottery, it is time for the firing. This is the final step. Firing the pottery makes the clay very strong so it will last for a long time.

My grandparents work together to build a kiln outside in the yard. They go out to the pasture and collect many pieces of dried cow manure. We call these "cow pies" because they are so flat and round. My grandparents lay some wood under a metal grate and put the pottery on top of it. They arrange the cow pies in a single layer on the top and sides of the pottery.

The cow pies are mostly made of grass, and they burn easily. They make the fire all around the pottery burn evenly at a very high

 April's grandmother rubs the bottom of a pot with a polishing stone that came to her from her mother. On her work table are bowls of red clay mixed with water and guaco.

temperature. We burn cow pies instead of wood because they do not contain pitch or sap that could stain the beautifully painted surfaces of the pottery.

After the fire is lit, we can only watch and wait. When the fire burns out and the pottery cools, my grandmother rakes the ashes away. We carefully remove the pottery and clean off any small bits of grit or ash. "Now the work is finished," my grandfather tells me proudly. "It is perfect and beautiful, made by our own hands from the earth's elements of fire, water, and clay."

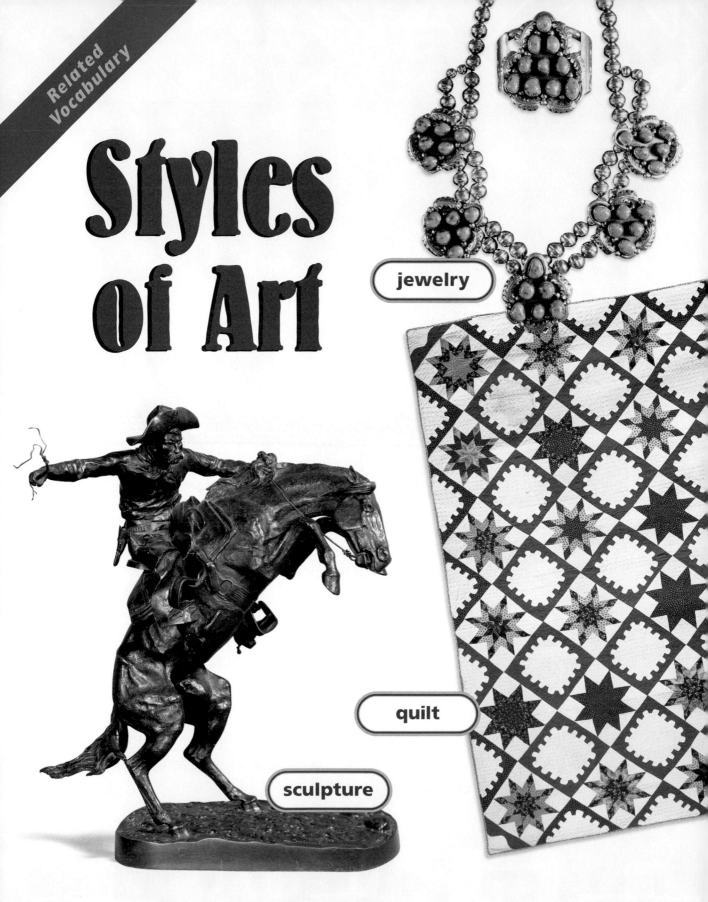

Styles of Art

jewelry

quilt

sculpture

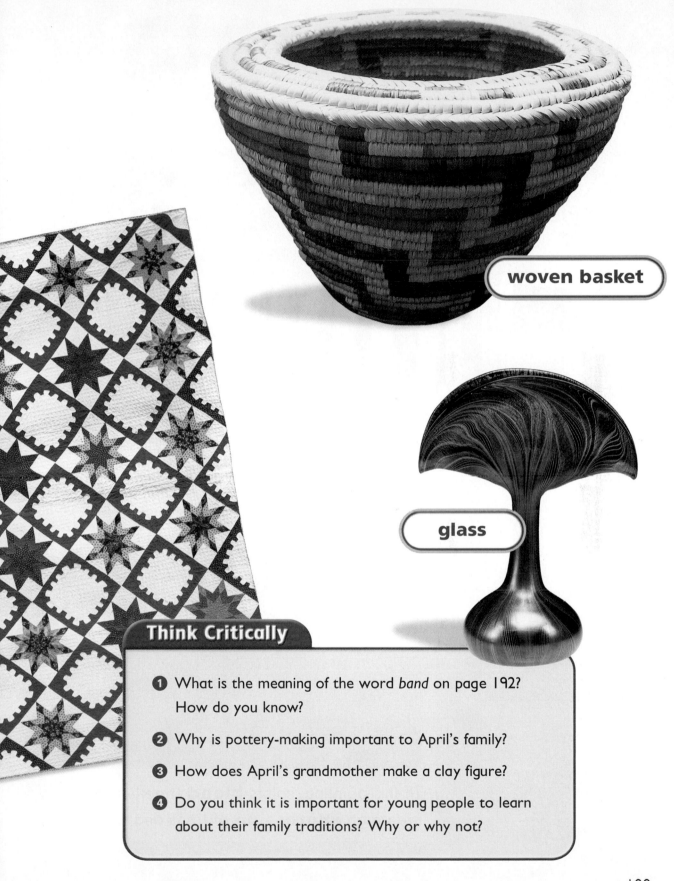

woven basket

glass

Think Critically

1 What is the meaning of the word *band* on page 192? How do you know?

2 Why is pottery-making important to April's family?

3 How does April's grandmother make a clay figure?

4 Do you think it is important for young people to learn about their family traditions? Why or why not?

199

Vocabulary POWER

Two Styles of Art ▼

VOCABULARY

compare

scenes

realistic

elements

impression

mood

contrast

blend

Compare the bottom of the painting to the top. The white boards of the fence **contrast** with the dark tree and sky.

In this painting, colors **blend** together to create an **impression** of trees and a field.

This is a **realistic** picture of a field.

The bright colors of these artists' **scenes** show a happy **mood**.

Color and shape are two of the **elements** of a painting.

Two Styles OF ART

In this selection, you will compare two paintings: *Promising Spring* by Konstantin Rodko and *Thatched Cottages at Cordeville* by Vincent van Gogh. The artists who painted them used different styles, or ways, to show things. The artists also used different kinds of colors.

Promising Spring by Konstantin Rodko

Thatched Cottages at Cordeville by Vincent van Gogh

Style

Rodko used bright and cheerful colors to paint objects. He painted things the way many people would see them. His art shows simple, familiar scenes. The scenes are realistic, but some elements of his paintings are unrealistic. For example, two of the trees in *Promising Spring* have blue leaves.

Van Gogh's style of painting is very different from Rodko's style. Van Gogh painted things the way he saw them. His paintings are his impression of how he saw them. His art shows objects that you might recognize, but in his paintings the objects don't look the way they do in real life.

◄ DETAIL 1

There are white, puffy clouds in the bright blue sky in *Promising Spring*. In *Thatched Cottages at Cordeville*, the sky is dark and heavy, and the clouds blend into the dark blue sky.

DETAIL 2 ►

Van Gogh's trees seem to flow together. This creates a dreamlike feeling. Rodko's trees are more colorful, and they stand apart from other objects in the painting.

◄ DETAIL 3

The door, windows, shutters, and porch railing of Rodko's pink house are easy to identify. In van Gogh's painting, it is hard to tell where the roof of one house ends and where the next roof begins.

Subject Matter

In *Promising Spring*, Rodko shows a farm and the people who work there. In *Thatched Cottages at Cordeville*, van Gogh shows houses in the country. Both paintings present familiar scenes from country life, but the paintings are very different. Van Gogh shows objects such as houses, trees, and clouds. Rodko includes people and animals doing different activities. In the foreground, or front of the scene, a man rakes leaves beneath a tree. In the background, or back of the scene, two men use horses to plow a field.

Color

In the painting by van Gogh, the artist shows his creativity by using many different shades of blue and green. Rodko's use of color is different from van Gogh's. He uses many bright colors to create a hopeful mood. The brightly colored farm buildings contrast with the green grass and brown soil. The pink house and the blue leaves on two trees show the painter's creativity.

Rodko's contrasting colors help show where one thing ends and another begins. Van Gogh's colors flow from one object to the next. This makes the objects appear to blend together.

Think Critically

1. How is Rodko's style different from van Gogh's style?

2. What time of day is it in each painting? What is the weather like in each painting? How can you tell?

3. How do van Gogh and Rodko show creativity in their paintings?

4. Which of these two paintings do you like better? Why?

Vocabulary POWER

Stories to Solve ▼

VOCABULARY

goat

cabbage

solution

thirsty

pitcher

edge

eldest

divide

fractions

pocket

One **goat** had a longer beard than the others. It was the **eldest** one.

In math class, we learned to **divide** large numbers. We wrote the answers in whole numbers and **fractions**.

We had to find the **solution** to each math problem. By the time I finished, I had filled my paper to the **edge**.

We were very **thirsty** after our long walk. My mother made a **pitcher** of lemonade.

The farmer planted a large field of **cabbage**.

This boy has his hand in his **pocket**.

Stories to Solve

FOLKTALES FROM AROUND THE WORLD

—

TOLD BY GEORGE SHANNON
ILLUSTRATED BY PETER SÍS

CROSSING THE RIVER

Once there was a man who had to take a wolf, a goat, and a cabbage across a river. But his boat was so small it could hold only himself and one other thing. The man didn't know what to do. How could he take the wolf, the goat, and the cabbage over one at a time, so that the wolf wouldn't eat the goat and the goat wouldn't eat the cabbage?

How It Was Done

Solution 1

He could take the goat over

and go back alone.

Then take the wolf over

and then bring the goat back.

Then take the cabbage over and leave the goat behind.

And finally make one last trip

and take the goat over
to join the wolf and cabbage.

Solution 2

He could take the goat over

and go back alone.

Then take the cabbage over

and bring the goat back.

Then take the wolf over and leave the goat behind.

And finally go back

and get the goat on the last trip.

A Drink for Crow

Once there was a crow who had grown so thirsty he could barely caw. He flew down to a big pitcher where he had gotten a drink of water the day before, but there was only a little bit of water remaining at the bottom. He tried and tried to reach it with his beak, but the pitcher was too deep and his beak was too short. But just as he was about to give up, he knew what to do. He flew back and forth from the garden to the pitcher until he was able to drink easily from the pitcher while sitting on its edge.

What did the crow do?

How It Was Done

The crow gathered pebbles, one by one, and dropped them into the pitcher until the water rose to the top.

DIVIDING THE HORSES

Once there lived a farmer, his wife, and their three sons. When the farmer died, his will said that the eldest son was to receive one-half of what he owned, the middle son was to receive one-third, and the youngest son was to receive one-ninth. All the farmer owned, however, was seventeen horses. And try as they might, the three sons could not figure out any way to divide the seventeen horses by their father's wishes.

"Don't worry," their mother told them. "We can solve this with a little help."

She went to the neighboring farm and borrowed a horse. Then with a total of eighteen horses, she gave the eldest son one-half, or nine horses. She gave the middle son one-third, or six of the horses. And she gave the youngest son one-ninth, or two of the horses.

"There," she said. "Nine plus six plus two makes the seventeen horses your father left you." And she returned the eighteenth horse to the neighbor.

How did she do it?

How It Was Done

1/2 plus 1/3 plus 1/9 does not equal one or all of anything.

The mother used their common denominator, which was eighteen, and changed the fractions to 9/18 plus 6/18 plus 2/18 which equaled 17/18.

So by borrowing the eighteenth horse she was creating a situation that matched the fractions.

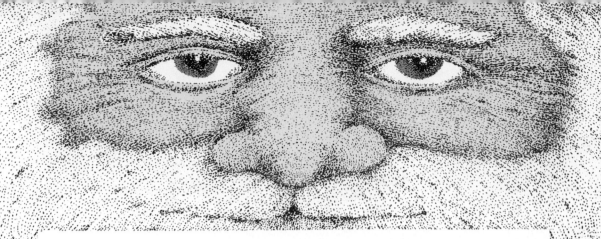

THE CLEVEREST SON

Once there lived an old man who had three sons. When he grew old and ill and knew that he soon would die, he called all three sons into his room.

"There is no way I can divide the house and farm to support all three of you. The one who proves himself the cleverest will inherit the house and farm. There is a coin on the table for each of you. The one who can buy something that will fill this room will inherit all I own."

The eldest son took his coin, went straight to the marketplace, and filled his wagon full of straw. The second son thought a bit longer, then also went to the marketplace, where he bought sacks and sacks of feathers. The youngest son thought and then quietly went to a little shop. He bought two small things and tucked them into his pocket.

That night the father called them in to show what they had bought. The eldest son spread his straw about the floor, but it filled only one part of the room. The second son dumped out his sacks of feathers, but they filled only two corners of the room. Then the youngest son smiled, pulled the two small things out of his pocket, and soon filled the room.

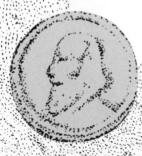

"Yes," said the father, "you are indeed the cleverest and have filled my room when the others could not. You shall inherit my house and farm."

What had the youngest son bought and with what did he fill the room?

How It Was Done

A match and a candle that filled the room with light.

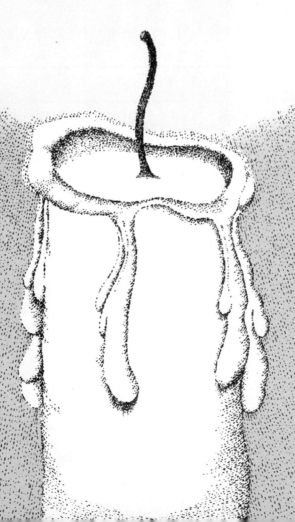

Famous Folktale · Characters ·

Lion and Mouse:
Greece

Spider:
West Africa

Tiger:
Korea

Rooster:
Mexico

Coyote:
Southwest United States

Think Critically

❶ Why doesn't the man cross the river with the wolf first?

❷ Describe the crow's problem.

❸ How else could the youngest son have filled the room?

❹ Which folktale did you like the best? Why?

Vocabulary POWER

Thomas Edison ▼

VOCABULARY

solve

problems

communicate

invent

improve

devices

create

images

Some people **create** art from things they find.

My uncle likes to **invent** new kinds of bikes.

I like long math **problems**. I work for hours to **solve** them.

Early cameras made only black-and-white **images**. Over the years, much has been done to **improve** cameras.

The light bulb is one of many **devices** invented by Thomas Edison.

In the 1800s, the telephone was a new way to **communicate**.

THOMAS EDISON

Thomas Edison was a creative inventor who worked hard to solve problems. Edison's inventions became very popular because they helped a lot of people.

Have you ever tried to read a book at night without an electric light? Could you listen to recorded music without a CD player or a cassette player? Thomas Edison's inventions made it easier for people to see things at night, listen to music, communicate with people far away, and much more.

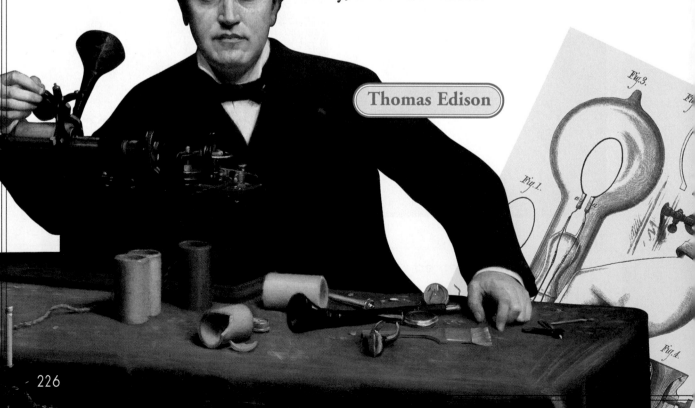

Thomas Edison

THE TELEGRAPH

When Thomas Edison was a boy, the telephone had not yet been invented. Computers did not exist, and there was no Internet. To communicate with family and friends who were far away, people had to use the mail or the telegraph.

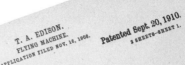

telegraph

The telegraph is a system that uses Morse code to send messages through an electrical wire. Morse code uses groups of short and long sounds to represent letters and numbers.

When he was fifteen, Edison got a job working as a telegraph operator, but what he really wanted to do was invent things and improve inventions that already existed.

At first, the telegraph could send or receive only one message at a time. Another inventor soon created a system that allowed a single wire to carry one message in each direction at the same time. Edison thought he could make this invention even better.

Edison came up with a solution. His improvement allowed two messages to be sent in each direction at the same time. Sending four messages at once over a single wire saved money and made communication faster.

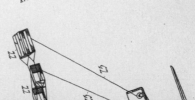

T. A. EDISON.
FLYING MACHINE.
APPLICATION FILED NOV. 18, 1908.

Patented Sept. 20, 1910.
2 SHEETS—SHEET 1.

970,616.

phonograph

THE PHONOGRAPH

Thomas Edison kept working to solve problems. He wanted to invent a machine that would record sounds and play them back.

Edison and a team of two helpers worked at his laboratory in Menlo Park, New Jersey. When Edison was ready to test his machine, he recited the rhyme "Mary Had a Little Lamb." The machine worked! It repeated what Edison had said.

Edison called his machine the phonograph. Soon people could listen to music and other kinds of recordings. A newspaper reporter called Edison "the Wizard of Menlo Park."

Over the years, other inventors improved the phonograph. Today there are many kinds of devices, such as the cassette player and the CD player, that can record and play back music.

THE LIGHT BULB

One of Edison's most famous inventions is the light bulb. In Edison's time, people did not use electric lights in their homes. They used gaslights, which were not very safe.

Some inventors had begun to make electric lights. For example, one inventor created a light that was good for streets at night. This light, however, was too bright to be used in homes. Edison was determined to make the electric light better.

One of the main problems was finding the right material for the filament—the thin wire inside a light bulb. "The Wizard of Menlo Park" tested over 1,600 different materials! Finally, he found just the right one.

Although Edison's light bulb worked well, he faced another problem. Houses and apartments did not have electricity. Lamps that used light bulbs could not be plugged in. Edison solved this problem, too. He created a system of making electricity and sending it to homes through wires.

Edison set up the first central station for electricity in New York City. Soon many other places were able to use light bulbs, too.

light bulb

THE KINETOSCOPE

Thomas Edison was becoming famous for his inventions. People all over the world used light bulbs and listened to music on the phonograph. However, Edison kept working on new inventions. He wanted to create a machine that would record and show moving pictures the way a phonograph recorded and played sounds.

After many experiments, Edison and his assistants did build a machine that recorded and showed moving pictures. He called his viewing machine a kinetoscope. It showed a series of images on a long roll of film. One person at a time could view these images through a small hole. The person would see people and things moving just as they do in modern movies. However, kinetoscope movies did not have any sound.

kinetoscope

The kinetoscope was very successful. People went to places that had coin-operated phonographs and kinetoscopes to listen to music and to watch short movies.

Other people improved Edison's inventions. In France, two brothers built a machine that showed a movie on a screen. This way many people could see the movie at once. The first movie theaters were called nickelodeons because the price to get in was a nickel.

Movie theaters today still use some of Edison's inventions. Electric light helps project the movie onto a screen. The movie projector uses technology that comes from both the kinetoscope and the phonograph. Do you think Edison ever imagined how important his inventions would become?

Think Critically

❶ How did each of Edison's inventions solve a problem?

❷ What would have happened if no one had improved the kinetoscope?

❸ How do Edison's inventions affect the way we live today?

❹ In your opinion, was Thomas Edison a creative person? Explain your answer.

Review Vocabulary with a Play

STORIES ON STAGE

JACK IS MISSING

Yumi Kim, 10

Mr. Kim, Yumi's father

Mrs. Kim, Yumi's mother

Jerry Kim, 14, Yumi's older brother

Margaret, 10, Yumi's classmate and friend

Mrs. Cooper, Neighbor

Mr. Pérez, Neighbor

Narrator

SCENE 1

Setting: The Kims' living room

Narrator: The living room is decorated for a birthday party. Everyone is singing "Happy Birthday" to Yumi.

Margaret: Make a wish, Yumi. Making a wish is one of my favorite birthday traditions.

Yumi: I wish…

Narrator: Yumi blows out the candles.

Everyone: Hooray! Hooray! Happy birthday!

Jerry: So, what did you wish for?

Yumi: I can't tell you. It's a secret.

Margaret: If she tells, then the wish won't come true.

Mr. Kim: Has anyone seen our dog, Jack?

Mrs. Kim: He was sitting by the fireplace just a minute ago.

Mr. Kim: Well, he's not there now. I don't see him.

Yumi: Jack, where are you?

Jerry: Here, boy! Here, boy!

Narrator: Everyone starts looking for Jack and calling out for him.

Mr. Kim: I don't think Jack is in the house.

Mrs. Kim: Maybe he went outside.

Yumi: Oh, no! This is going to be a sad birthday party.

Jerry: Don't worry, Yumi. We'll find Jack. Stay in your happy mood. All of us are good at solving problems.

Margaret: I have an idea. Why don't we put Jack's favorite food on the porch? Maybe he'll smell it and come to eat it.

Mrs. Kim: That may be the solution. I'll go get his favorite food and his bowl.

Narrator: Mrs. Kim puts the food on the porch. Everyone begins calling out for Jack again.

Yumi: I don't think this is working.

Jerry: I have an idea. Let's ask the neighbors if they saw Jack.

Mrs. Kim: That's a great idea. We'll go together.

Mr. Kim: I'll stay here in case Jack comes back.

SCENE 2

Setting: Mrs. Cooper's house

Narrator: Mrs. Kim, Jerry, Yumi, and Margaret walk next door to Mrs. Cooper's house. Mrs. Kim knocks on the door. Mrs. Cooper answers.

Mrs. Cooper: Hello, Mrs. Kim. Hello, children. Why do you look so upset? Is there a problem?

Mrs. Kim: Yes, Mrs. Cooper. Our dog, Jack, is missing. Have you seen him?

Mrs. Cooper: I'm sorry. I haven't seen him today, but I'll call you if I do.

Yumi: Thank you, Mrs. Cooper.

Setting: Mr. Pérez's house

Narrator: The group goes to Mr. Pérez's house next. They knock on his door, and he answers.

Mr. Pérez: Hello, Mrs. Kim. Hello, children. Is everything okay?

Mrs. Kim: No, Mr. Pérez. Our dog, Jack, is missing. Have you seen him?

Mr. Pérez: No, I haven't seen him. I'll call you if I do.

Jerry: I don't think my idea of asking the neighbors is working.

Yumi: I have an idea. I put Jack's favorite squeaky toy in my pocket before we left. Maybe if he hears it, he'll come to us.

Narrator: The group walks around, squeezing the toy and calling Jack. After a while, they stop.

Yumi: I don't think he can hear his toy.

Mrs. Kim: Let's go home. Maybe Jack is back.

Setting: The Kims' living room

Scene 4

Mr. Kim: Did you find Jack?

Margaret: No, and Mrs. Cooper and Mr. Pérez haven't seen him either.

Jerry: Yumi squeaked Jack's favorite toy, but he didn't hear it.

Margaret: Look! The tablecloth is moving!

Narrator: Yumi lifts up the tablecloth.

Yumi: It's Jack! He's under the table! Jack, we were so worried about you!

Mr. Kim: I have the impression that he never left the house.

Yumi: That was a hard mystery to solve! Now let's cut that birthday cake!

Review Activities

Think and Respond

1 How are people who paint and people who make pottery alike? How are they different?

2 Why do you think April enjoys making Storyteller dolls with her grandparents?

3 Whose painting style do you like better, van Gogh's or Rodko's? Why?

4 How was the problem solved in "Dividing the Horses?" What other creative problem solvers did you read about in this unit?

5 How did Thomas Edison's improvement of the telegraph help people to communicate?

LANGUAGE STRUCTURE REVIEW

Describe Surroundings

Create a short list of questions about a room in a home, such as

- What room is it?
- What color is the room?

Ask a partner to think of a room in his or her home. Use your list of questions to ask him or her about the room. Write down your partner's answers. Then use your notes to describe his or her room to your classmates.

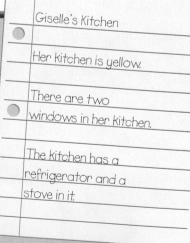

Giselle's Kitchen

Her kitchen is yellow.

There are two windows in her kitchen.

The kitchen has a refrigerator and a stove in it.

Fill in the Blank

Form small groups with your classmates. Each group will need the Vocabulary Cards for this unit and some index cards. Choose a Vocabulary Card. On an index card, write a sentence using the word you picked. Leave a blank where that word would go.

Shuffle the Vocabulary Cards and the index cards. Lay all the cards on the table, and work with your group to match words with sentences.

language

What _____ do you speak?

thirsty

I'm very _____.
I need a drink.

apartment building

shop

Deli Store

240

SING ALONG

This Community

With its homes,
Shops, and schools,
Playgrounds, parks, and
Swimming pools,
With police to keep you safe—
Firefighters, too—
This community's for you!

*Sing to the tune of
"This Old Man."*

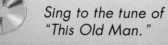

park

241

Fact and Opinion

A **fact** is a statement that can be proven. An **opinion** is a statement about a person's ideas or beliefs. An opinion cannot be proven to be true. Some words show a person's opinion, such as *think, believe, feel,* and *should.*

Read the paragraph. Then look at the chart to see which statements are facts and which are opinions.

I think that firefighters have a very important job. Their job is to keep people in the community safe. Firefighters do dangerous work. Sometimes they risk their lives to save other people. I believe that firefighters are very brave. Everyone should respect and appreciate the job they do.

Facts	Opinions
Their job is to keep people in the community safe.	I think that firefighters have a very important job.
Firefighters do dangerous work.	I believe that firefighters are very brave.
Sometimes they risk their lives to save other people.	Everyone should respect and appreciate the job they do.

Try This

▶ Read the paragraph. On a separate sheet of paper, copy
the fact-and-opinion chart. Use the information in the
paragraph below to complete the chart.

I believe that the public library is the most important
part of a community. Public libraries provide free
information. People can borrow
books to learn about many
subjects. Many libraries have
computers that are connected
to the Internet. The public
library is a great place.
Everyone should visit it.

Facts	Opinions

Colonial Conversations ▼

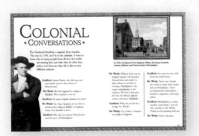

VOCABULARY

reporter

colonies

freedom

beliefs

community

industries

trade

opportunities

flood

merchants

A **reporter** on television said that the heavy rains would **flood** the streets.

People sailed to the American **colonies** in the 1700s. Many of them were in search of **freedom**.

Americans today share many **beliefs** about freedom.

People created new **industries** all over the United States. Often a **community** grew up around a factory and a river.

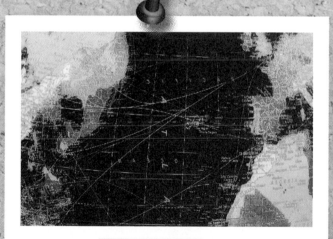

American **merchants** sold items such as corn, sugar, and cotton. People in the shipping **trade** carried these items around the world.

The Statue of Liberty is a symbol that stands for the **opportunities** people can find in the United States.

COLONIAL
◆ CONVERSATIONS ◆

I'm Chadwick Hardford, a reporter from London. The year is 1750, and I'm in the colonies. I want to learn why so many people from all over the world are moving here and what they do after they arrive. Let's find out what life is like in two different colonies.

Hardford: Martin Wooly, why did you and your family move to the colony of Pennsylvania?

Mr. Wooly: We left England for religious freedom. We're Quakers, you see.

Hardford: Do many English Quakers live here?

Mr. Wooly: Yes. Since Quakers are not free to practice their religious beliefs in England, many of us decided to leave.

Hardford: Why did you choose Pennsylvania and the town of Philadelphia?

In 1750, immigrants from England, Wales, Germany, Scotland, Ireland, Holland, and France lived in Philadelphia.

Mr. Wooly: William Penn was an English Quaker. He founded Pennsylvania and made it a place where we are free to worship. Philadelphia is the largest community in the colonies. We have a fine port, the first free library, lighted streets, and many industries.

Hardford: What do you do for a living, Mr. Wooly?

Mr. Wooly: I'm a baker. I learned my trade in England.

Hardford: You must do very well. Everyone needs bread.

Mr. Wooly: That's true. People also work in many other trades here in Philadelphia. There are blacksmiths, shoemakers, butchers, carpenters, and many others.

Hardford: Philadelphia is a busy, modern community. I can see why you like it, Mr. Wooly. Thank you for speaking with me.

Mr. Wooly: You're welcome.

A Carolina rice field

Now I'm in a southern colony, South Carolina. Let's talk to one of the plantation owners here.

Hardford: Mrs. Claudia Hoffman and her husband own a large rice plantation in a community not far from Charles Town, South Carolina. Mrs. Hoffman, why did you and your husband come here from Germany?

Mrs. Hoffman: We came because there are many opportunities here. We knew we could make a good living in South Carolina.

Hardford: Why did you decide to grow rice?

Mrs. Hoffman: Most of the people in this community are rice farmers. You see, the river isn't far away. That means there are many marshes. Wet, marshy land is perfect for growing good rice. Rice is the most important crop in South Carolina.

Hardford: Is it difficult to grow?

Mrs. Hoffman: Yes, it's very difficult. First, we have to flood the rice fields with water. We leave the water on the plants for a while, and then we drain it. This is very hot, wet work, and there are many mosquitoes.

Hardford: What happens to the rice that you grow?

Mrs. Hoffman: It is loaded onto wagons. My husband and other workers take the rice to Charles Town to sell it.

Hardford: Charles Town seems to be an important place for business.

Mrs. Hoffman: Oh, yes. There are many merchants in Charles Town. The port makes it the richest community in the South.

Hardford: What do people do in Charles Town for fun?

Mrs. Hoffman: The theater is very popular. The Dock Street Theater in Charles Town was one of the first in the colonies.

Hardford: Charles Town sounds like an interesting community. Thank you, Mrs. Hoffman. Good luck with your crop this year.

Mrs. Hoffman: Thank you.

Think Critically

❶ Does the sentence *William Penn was an English Quaker.* express a fact or an opinion? How could you check your answer?

❷ Why did many people settle in the colonies in the 1700s?

❸ Why were Philadelphia and Charles Town important colonial communities?

❹ Would you have enjoyed living in the colonies? Explain your answer.

Vocabulary POWER

Welcome to Chinatown ▼

VOCABULARY

tourists

ancestors

century

settled

immigrated

restaurants

discover

parade

It's fun to eat in **restaurants**. There are many new foods to **discover**.

My **ancestors** lived in China. They helped build this temple more than a **century** ago.

My grandparents **immigrated** to the United States before my parents were born. They **settled** in San Francisco, California, and still live there.

Tourists are people who travel to a place just to visit. They often take pictures during their trip.

We stood on the sidewalk as the **parade** of soldiers with flags marched by.

WELCOME
TO
CHINATOWN

HISTORY OF CHINATOWN

Every year many tourists visit San Francisco, California. A lot of them want to see a special part of the city, called Chinatown. Chinatown is a community in the middle of San Francisco.

Most of the people who live in this community have ancestors from China. San Francisco is not the only city with a Chinatown. New York, Chicago, and Boston also have Chinatowns.

San Francisco's Chinatown began in the nineteenth century. By the 1840s many Chinese people had settled in the United States. Some lived near one another in central San Francisco. In their community they spoke Chinese and followed Chinese traditions. In later years tens of thousands of Chinese people immigrated to the United States. Many decided to live in San Francisco's Chinese community, which soon was called Chinatown.

WHAT TO SEE AND DO

Chinatown is a popular spot for tourists because it has many things to see and do. Remember to take a camera if you go there!

The best way to see Chinatown is by walking. You know you're there when you walk under the Chinatown gate.

Chinatown is a great place to shop. Along the crowded streets, stores sell Chinese clothing, toys, games, art, food, and books. Do you like kites? Several shops sell beautiful, colorful Chinese kites.

The Chinatown gate welcomes visitors to this colorful and interesting community. ▶

▲ **Chinatown in San Francisco, California**

Chinatown is also home to the Chinese Cultural Center. There you can watch a film about China or take a Chinese cooking class. You can also just look around at many amazing things from China.

WHAT TO EAT

The delicious food is one thing that brings many people to Chinatown. You will find many restaurants along the busy main streets.

What will you eat in Chinatown? It's up to you! The menus in most Chinese restaurants are long because they offer so many choices. There are all kinds of things to eat with rice. You'll find vegetables, beef, pork, chicken, duck, and seafood. Most meals come with Chinese tea. If you're not very hungry, try a bowl of delicious hot and sour soup.

▲ **Shops and street stands in Chinatown sell many kinds of food.**

Restaurants aren't the only places to get good food in Chinatown. Along the streets are many shops and stands that sell fresh food. Stop and take a look at them. You will probably discover some kinds of food that you've never seen before. If you're tired of walking, take a break at a Chinese bakery and enjoy a delicious almond cookie!

◀ **In a Chinese restaurant, you can eat with chopsticks.**

A COMMUNITY

Whenever you walk through Chinatown, you'll notice that it's not just a place for tourists. It's a real community full of people who live and work there. In Chinatown, children go to school and adults go to work. You'll see people going to worship in temples and churches. If you're lucky, maybe you'll see a parade. You'll see older people sitting together and talking. Some of these people have lived and worked in Chinatown their whole lives.

This special community is a wonderful place to discover Chinese culture in America.

▲ **Thousands of people live and work in the Chinatown community.**

▼ **Chinatown in San Francisco is a place that tourists remember.**

CHINESE FOOD

vegetables

soy sauce

egg rolls

shrimp chow mein

beef and broccoli

rice

tea

wonton soup

Think Critically

❶ What are some things to see and do in Chinatown?

❷ How is Chinatown like your own community? How is it different?

❸ Why do you think so many people like to visit Chinatown?

❹ Would you like to visit Chinatown one day? Why or why not?

257

Vocabulary POWER

We buy our fruit at this **supermarket**. The **business** does very well because the fruit is so fresh.

Grandpa's Corner Store ▼

VOCABULARY

supermarket

counter

neighbors

construction

delivery

business

worried

flyer

The toppings for the ice cream are on the **counter**.

Our new **neighbors**, who live across the street, welcomed us to the neighborhood.

Our mail **delivery** was early today. The mail carrier gave us a **flyer** showing the new hours for the post office.

The **construction** work on this house will not be finished until next month.

This actress is pretending to be **worried** about something.

Grandpa's Corner Store

by DyAnne DiSalvo-Ryan

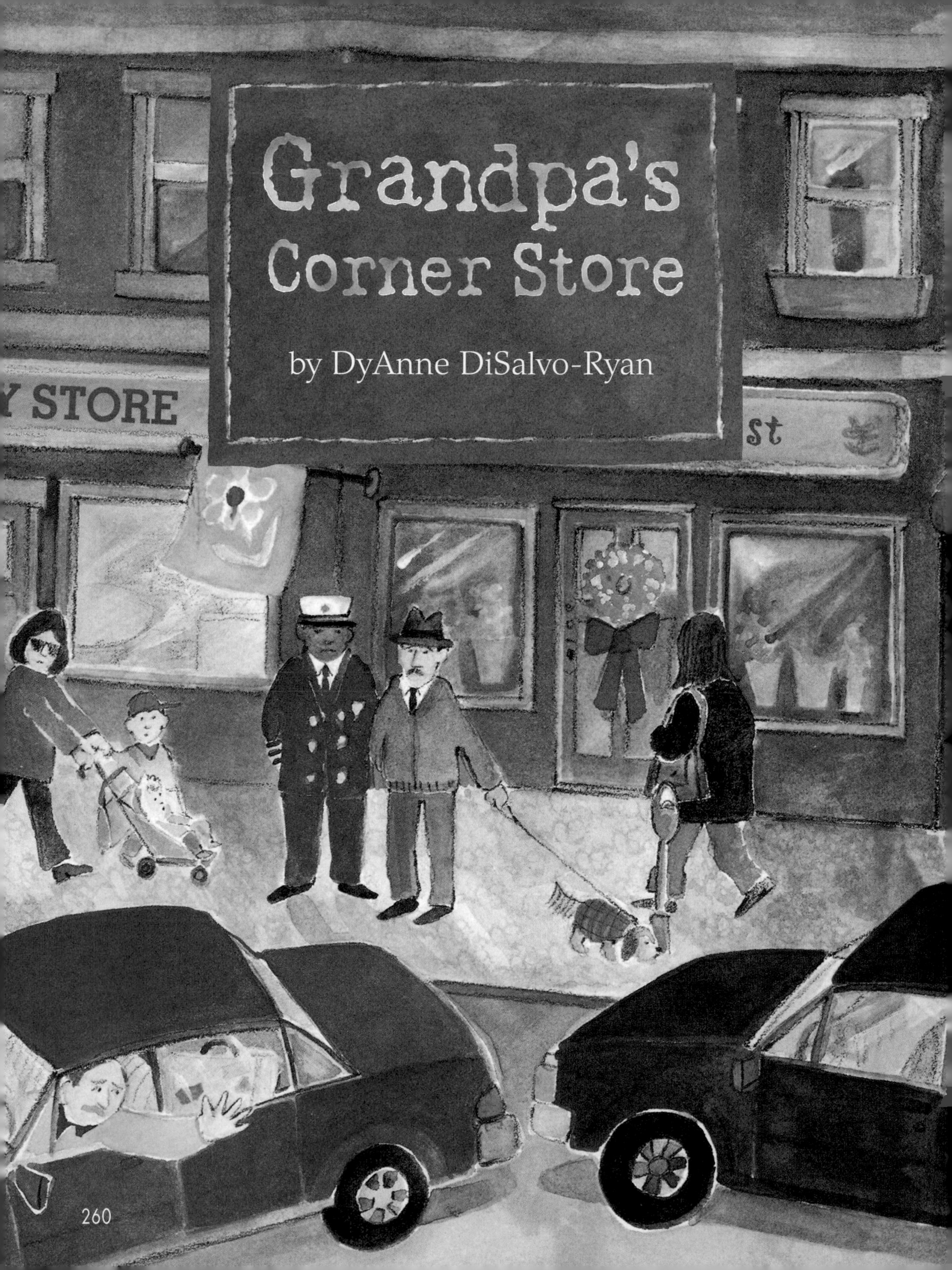

M̲r. Butler sold his hardware store when a bigger one opened nearby. Then the building was torn down to make way for a new supermarket.

"Good luck," I say to Mr. Butler as he bumps his suitcase into his car.

"We'll miss you," my grandpa tells him. "*And* we'll miss your hardware store."

I hold on to Grandpa's hand, and we wave until Mr. Butler's car turns the corner.

Old stores are out. New stores are in. But my grandpa's store stays the same. A busy corner grocery with black and white tiles all worn straight down the middle aisle. Milk, juice, butter, eggs—the store has everything you need close by.

Grandpa lives in a room in the back. There's a bed for sleeping, a kitchen for cooking, and a cat named Shirley for company.

Saturday mornings I'm at the grocery to give Grandpa a hand. I stack the cans and sweep the aisles. Kids toss their bikes and skateboards outside and pile inside for candy. Firefighters from across the street line up at the deli counter. Mrs. Kalfo takes their orders and bags them up to go.

"I know, I know," Mrs. Kalfo says. "Cheese and pickle sandwiches. Hers on rye. His on wheat. Extra mayo on yours, right, chief?"

Chief Conley smiles at Grandpa. "She always gets it right."

The store is busy on Saturdays, so my mother comes in to help. Neighbors stop by to pick up what they need—a quart of milk, a box of cereal. Mr. Tutti comes in for yesterday's paper. He likes to take his time when he reads, so Grandpa saves it for him.

"So what do you think? With the new supermarket opening up, are you going to sell your store?" Mr. Tutti says flat out to my grandpa.

"Sell the grocery?" I look at Grandpa. "I don't think so," I tell Mr. Tutti. "My grandpa would never do that."

On Monday morning my teacher, Miss McCartney, tapes our neighborhood map on the board. We paste the library closest to the school, Korina's house farthest from Ira's.

"The new supermarket will have everything," Steven says without even raising his hand.

"My grandpa's store has everything already," I say a little bit louder than Miss McCartney would like.

But whatever I say that Grandpa's store has, Steven says the supermarket will have it too. Cheaper and bigger and better.

After school I stop for a minute to watch the construction work. My ears begin to tingle from the noise. Then all of a sudden I get this feeling that maybe Steven is right. The supermarket *is* going to be big. It was already much bigger than me.

"Lucy's here," Grandpa yells, waiting to give me my three o'clock hug. Mrs. Kalfo takes charge of the register. The table in the kitchen is set for homework, and Grandpa keeps me company. My mother says it's a nice arrangement to have while she's at work. I think so too.

"I'm making your corner grocery store to put on the neighborhood map at school," I say. Grandpa watches me color it in. "Steven is making the supermarket. He says your store is all washed up and you'll be moving to Florida, just like Mr. Butler."

Grandpa sighs and picks up a crayon. "Maybe Florida is nice," he says. "It's not so cold in the winter."

I laugh and give Grandpa a kiss. "Florida's too far away. You can't run your store from there."

When the telephone rings, it's Mr. Lee calling in an order.

"He's under the weather," my grandpa says.

I help pack the delivery bag. Bread, soup, coffee, noodles. Grandpa puts his coat on to go. Some deliveries are special, so he likes to do them himself.

I've finished coloring Grandpa's store when my mother comes to get me. I toss my crayons under the counter just before I leave. That's when I see a red FOR SALE sign hidden beneath some bags.

I can't even talk on the way home, but when we get inside, the words spill out.

"Is Grandpa selling his store?" I ask.

My mother sits us both in a chair. "Grandpa doesn't *want* to sell. He's afraid the new supermarket will put him out of business."

"Will Grandpa live with us if he sells?"

My mother looks around. "I'd like that more than anything," she says. "But we don't have the room."

I am just about to say he can have my room when I hear a knock at the door. Mrs. Kalfo stands in the hallway.

"Everybody's talking," Mrs. Kalfo says. She flutters her hands like a bird in a nest. "Everybody's worried the store will close."

"We're worried too," my mother says. "Come in. Sit down."

Mrs. Kalfo straightens her hat. "I guess, if it does, I'll try to get a job at the new supermarket. Things won't be the same for me anymore."

I throw my arms around my mother. "We have to do something," I say.

The next day, on the way to Grandpa's store, I try not to notice that the supermarket's going up fast. Construction workers call out to one another, waving steel beams into place. The sky is gray and thick with clouds. It almost feels like snow.

"Cold out there?" Mrs. Kalfo asks me, wrapping up a sandwich. Mrs. Duffy from down the block is huddled up talking to Grandpa.

"Pay when you can," I hear Grandpa whisper. Cheese, milk, diapers, bread.

Mrs. Duffy pats Grandpa's hand. "What would I do without you?" she says.

I bring my homework into the back and wait at the kitchen table.

As soon as Grandpa takes his seat, I ask him about that
FOR SALE sign.

Grandpa looks down at the black and white tiles that need
to be replaced. He looks up at a crack in the ceiling that needs
to be repaired. "The new supermarket will have everything from
soup to nuts," he tells me.

"But it won't have *you*." I hug my grandpa, trying not to cry.
I give him the grocery store I colored in for school. "If you're
really going to sell your store, then you can keep this," I say.
"The map won't need it now."

The Saturday the roof goes up on the supermarket, the FOR SALE sign goes up in Grandpa's window. In school on Monday, I won't even look at Steven. He keeps waving around a flyer he ripped from a pole on the avenue—

SUPERMARKET OPENS NEXT WEEK.

"I hope your grandpa likes Florida," he says, teasing. I grab the flyer out of his hand and throw it into the wastebasket.

We take turns pasting up more buildings. Somebody puts a tag with the words *mud pile* where the supermarket is being built, but Miss McCartney takes it down. I think that somebody is me.

"A community is a group of people who live and work together," Miss McCartney says, pointing to our map.

I think about what our community would be like without my grandpa's store.

And then I look at Steven and smile. Miss McCartney has given me an idea.

272

"Be there Saturday morning,"
I tell all the kids on my way
home after school.

"Nine o'clock sharp," the
firefighters say.

"I'll help spread the word,"
says Mr. Tutti.

"Not a problem." Mr. Lee
sneezes.

Mrs. Kalfo pats my arm. "You
can count on me," she says.

It snows every single day that week. Clouds hang frozen in the winter sky like sheets dried stiff on a clothesline. But that doesn't stop the supermarket from opening up on Saturday. Colored flags snap in the wind. SPECIAL! SPECIAL! SALE TODAY! My mother and I yank on boots, pull down hats, and head for Grandpa's store.

"I hope this works," I tell my mother as we brave our way around the corner.

Neighbors are bunched in front of the grocery all packed up like snowballs.

"Here comes Lucy!" Chief Conley waves.

Mr. Lee is pouring out coffee. Mrs. Duffy has her five kids bundled up onto a sled.

Mrs. Kalfo is laughing. "Your grandpa can't see us. His windows are all iced up."

There's the carpenter's truck, the kids from school—even Miss McCartney's here.

I take a deep breath and push the door open.

"Where is everybody?" I ask Grandpa, trying to keep the secret.

"Probably at the supermarket," he says. "Who needs this place now?"

"You'd be surprised," I tell my grandpa.

That's when the old front door claps open, cheering for everyone as they come in. Neighbors are carrying paint cans, black and white tiles, nails and hammers, and plaster mix. Some of the people I don't even know.

"What's all this?" my grandpa asks.

"It's Lucy's idea," Mrs. Kalfo says. "We're all here to spruce up this place."

"Did you really think we'd let you get away so fast?" Chief Conley asks my grandpa.

"Who's going to make my deliveries special?" Mr. Lee wants to know.

"And what about our cheese and pickle sandwiches?" the firefighters remind Grandpa.

"And you know me," Mr. Tutti says. "I need yesterday's news today."

"Do you still want this?" I ask Grandpa, taking down the FOR SALE sign.

Grandpa looks around his store. People keep coming in left and right, banging their feet, rubbing their hands, and getting to work. Grandpa walks into the kitchen and comes out holding my colored-in grocery store.

"Thank you, Lucy," he whispers, handing it back to me. "I think your map will need this now." Then Grandpa hugs me, broom and all.

Well, the grand opening of the supermarket was a huge success. Steven was right. The supermarket is big. But it isn't bigger than a whole neighborhood.

In school Steven pastes a big rectangle on our map and marks it "supermarket."

I raise my hand. "Bigger but not better," I tell Miss McCartney. Then I paste my grandpa's grocery store right around the corner from my house. Milk, juice, butter, eggs—it has everything you need close by. And best of all, it has Grandpa.

At the Supermarket

produce

dairy

household products

deli

breads and cereals

FROSTED TOASTED OATS
toasted oat cereal

CRACKERS
4 Stack Packs
NET WT. 16 OZ (1 LB) 454g

OLD FASHIONED OATS
100% Natural

ZITI • 2
ENRICHED MACARONI PRODUCT

EXTRA LARGE

Superior
EXTRA LARGE

Think Critically

1 How does the community work together to save Grandpa's corner store?

2 How does Lucy feel when she thinks Grandpa might close the store?

3 How do you think the author feels about small community grocery stores? How do you know?

4 What is something that people in your community could do to make your neighborhood better?

Vocabulary POWER

Nature's Great Balancing Act ▼

VOCABULARY

creatures

mammal

reptiles

energy

populations

balance

territory

burrow

Alligators are interesting **creatures**. These **reptiles** live in swamps and marshy areas.

The whale is a **mammal**. It is warm-blooded and breathes air.

There are many ways to collect **energy**. Windmills collect energy from the wind.

The animal **populations** of a **territory** may include many different kinds of animals.

These owls live in a **burrow** in the ground for shelter.

Gymnasts must have good **balance** so that they will not fall while performing.

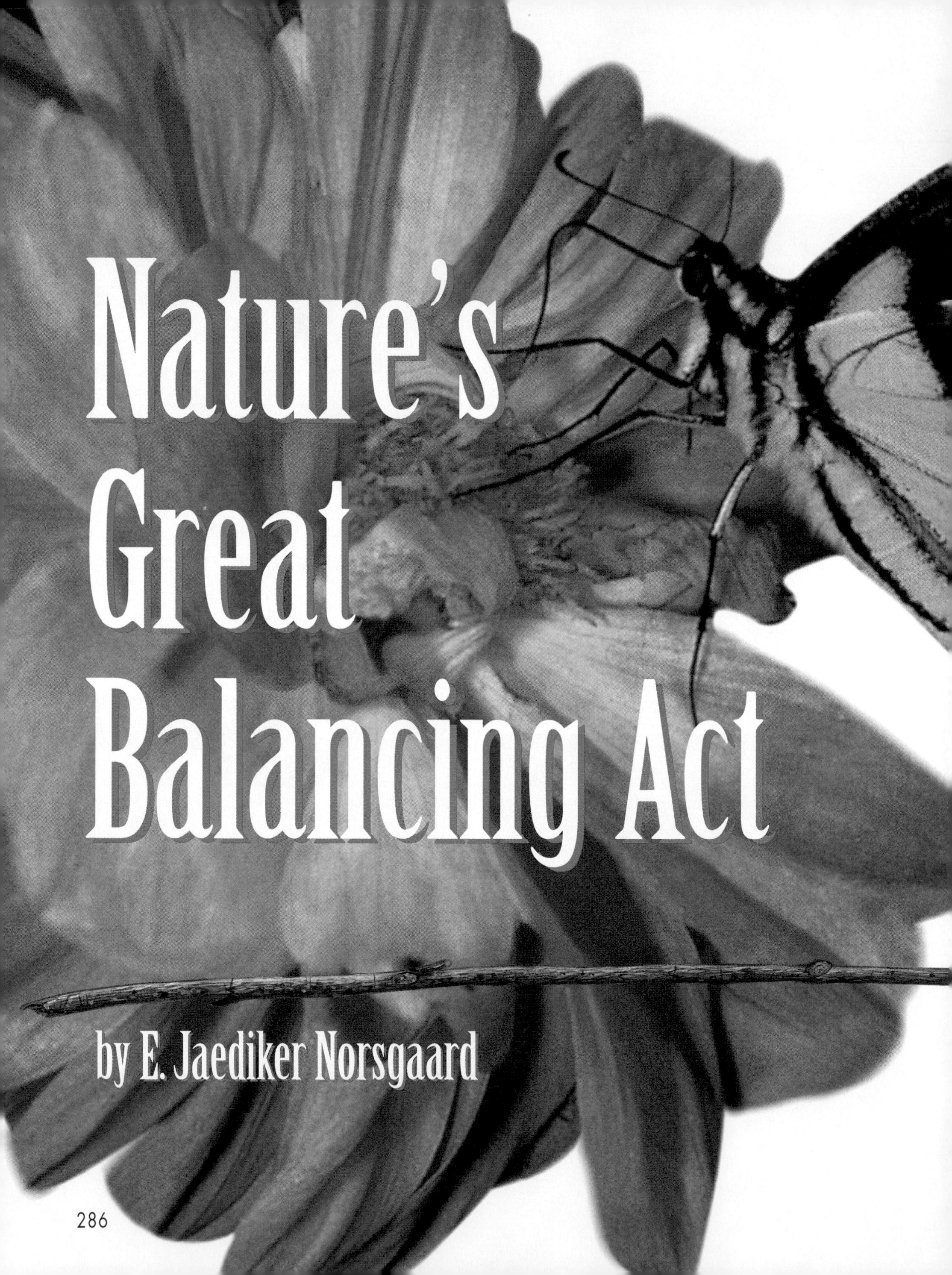

Nature's Great Balancing Act

by E. Jaediker Norsgaard

Welcome to our backyard!

You won't find a tame grass carpet, but a large semi-wild wonderland that stretches from our house to the bordering woods. Some years ago we decided to let everything grow as it pleases. Now it's a community where many of our fellow creatures are at home. On a summer day, grasshoppers will jump away from your footsteps.

You'll see bees buzzing around raspberry bushes, butterflies landing on wildflowers, birds feeding insects to their young. There are chipmunks and a family of bold raccoons. Deer venture out of the woods to nibble hedges and shrubs.

All creatures in the animal kingdom depend on plants and on each other for survival, one feeding on another. They are all parts of a gigantic puzzle in which the pieces fit together but, like a kaleidoscope, are forever changing. You are a mammal, and you are a part of that puzzle too, though you are quite different from other mammals and from birds, reptiles, amphibians, and insects. All living things are members of nature's great balancing act. You can see how this works right here in our own backyard.

Food Chains

Nature's great balancing act depends on food chains. All food chains begin with plants. Plants are able to make their own food, using energy from the sun, and they pass that energy on to animals that eat them. Plants are the basis of all the food and energy that you and other animals use.

When an animal eats a plant or eats another animal, it becomes part of a food chain. In our backyard, as well as everywhere else, all food chains begin with plant-eaters (herbivores) and usually end with a meat-eater (carnivore). Food chains can be short or as long as five or six links. If you eat an apple, that is a two-link food chain. If you eat meat from a sheep or cow that has eaten plants, that is a three-link food chain. You are at the top of those food chains.

Here in the backyard, one food chain might begin with a moth sipping nectar from a flower. The moth is caught by a sparrow and fed to its young in the nest in our hedge. The young bird might be taken from its nest and eaten by a raccoon. The raccoon is at the top of this food chain. There are no predators in the backyard to eat the raccoon.

Another food chain might start with a fly feeding on decaying vegetation in the backyard. The fly is caught and eaten by a spider. The spider is eaten by a toad, which is eaten by a fox.

Red fox

First links in any food chain are usually the smallest but most abundant plants and animals. Microscopic green algae and other plant plankton float in the ponds, lakes, and seas. They are eaten in great quantities by water insects and small crustaceans, which are eaten by small fishes, which are, in turn, eaten by larger fishes that may end up on your dinner table.

Each time an animal eats a plant or one animal eats another, a tiny bit of the sun's energy is passed along the food chain. Each animal uses some of that energy and passes along what is left. Amazingly, the used energy is not destroyed, only changed into other forms or passed into the atmosphere.

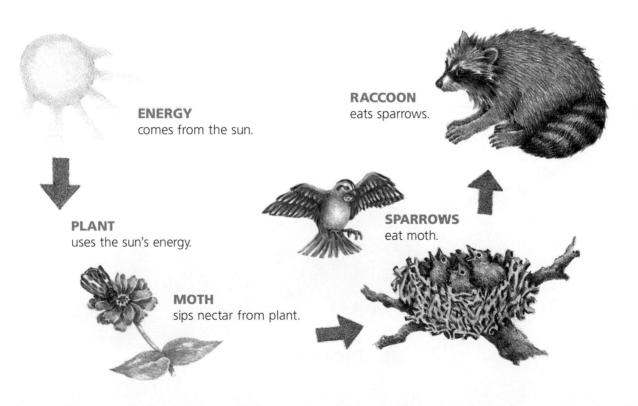

ENERGY
comes from the sun.

RACCOON
eats sparrows.

PLANT
uses the sun's energy.

SPARROWS
eat moth.

MOTH
sips nectar from plant.

Balancing Populations

Animal populations are kept in balance by the amount of food available and by predators in the food chain. Take mice, for instance. You can't really catch sight of them scurrying through the tall grass in the backyard, eating seeds. They move quickly to avoid enemies. During a summer of heavy rainfall and lush vegetation, the mouse population increases, providing more food for hawks and owls and other mouse-eaters. When less food is available, mice tend to raise fewer young. This affects the numbers of hawks and owls also. If the insect and rodent populations decrease, owls and hawks raise fewer young or find better territory or else starve. A balance of numbers is maintained.

 mouse

owl

Some farmers shoot hawks and owls, believing that they kill a few chickens. But without these predators, rabbits and mice overpopulate and spread into cultivated fields to eat corn, wheat, oats, rye, barley, rice, and sugar cane—the grasses which are first links in human food chains. This is what happens when we upset a balanced community.

Feathered Helpers

Birds are a great help in keeping the numbers of insects in balance.

The friendly chickadees are greeting us from the lilac bushes, with their cheerful call . . . dee-dee-dee . . . between dashes to the feeder for sunflower seeds, or into the brush for caterpillars and other insects and spiders.

A couple of barn swallows are catching winged insects to feed their babies in a mud-and-straw nest on a high beam in our garden tool shed.

A pair of cardinals is swooping down on grasshoppers. I can't help hoping that no snake or owl raids their nest in the hedge, but that's a possibility.

The tiny house wren parents are tireless hunters, making continuous trips from dawn until dark to satisfy the high-pitched hunger cries of their babies in the nest box near our kitchen window. A young bird may eat its weight in insects every day!

In the spring, we watch the birds compete for inchworms, hopping from twig to twig, picking the leaves clean.

We saw the female Baltimore oriole peel dried fibers off last year's tall dogbane plant with her beak and fly high up in the oak tree to weave them into her nest. She and the

 barn swallows

young blue jay

male who courted and won her fed their nestlings with soft parts of insects, and themselves ate caterpillars, beetles, wasps, grasshoppers, and ants.

Young blue jays with innocent faces and fresh white and blue feathers follow their parents around, fluttering their wings to be fed, although they've grown as large as the adults.

Birds are a joy to watch as they go about their business, protecting the plants in our backyards and gardens from an oversupply of leaf-eating insects.

grasshopper

Mammals

A family of deer often comes out of the small woods bordering our backyard and browses among the plants. When we go outside, they stop and stare at us with wide eyes, then turn and leap gracefully away, wiggling their white tails.

In winter, they walk through the snow up to the house itself to nibble hedges and shrubs. Deer can double their numbers in a single year. Long ago, their populations were kept in check mainly by cougars (mountain lions) that leaped on them from low tree limbs. And by packs of wolves, and by native American Indians who hunted them for food, buckskins, and doeskins. Today, without predators except man in many places, deer sometimes eat every leaf and bud in their range, and some starve in winter.

family of deer

The lively little chipmunks have found an easy way to make a living. Besides collecting wild plant seeds, one is sitting near the bird feeder, stuffing so many fallen sunflower seeds into his mouth that the pouches in his cheeks puff up like small balloons. He races to his underground nest to store them away and is soon back for more, running quickly to avoid hawks and other predators.

chipmunk

tree cricket

A red fox sometimes walks stealthily into our backyard at sunset, hunting mice and birds. The chipmunks dart into their burrow where they're safe from the fox, but not from the weasels.

As we wait for more furry visitors, the evening air is filled with scraping sounds of katydids calling their own names, and the high jingle bell chorus of snowy tree crickets. They feed on the foliage in which they hide, daring to advertise for mates at night when the birds that prey on them are asleep.

katydid

A family of raccoons and an opossum make trails through the backyard, stopping to munch berries. This is part of their regular rounds as they seek out mice, lizards, grasshoppers, and crickets, and grub in the mud for frogs.

raccoon

opossum

 frog

In case they're still hungry, the raccoons are bold enough to look in our kitchen window or tap on the door and invite themselves in for a snack. The opossum, who eats almost anything, gets in on the act. After all, humans have taken over much of their territory.

Think Critically

1. How do different kinds of animals "balance" one another?

2. What would happen if there were no birds in the backyard? How do you know?

3. How are plants and the sun connected in a food chain?

4. Would you like to have a backyard like the one you read about? Why or why not?

LESSON 25 Unit Review

Review Vocabulary with a Play

STORIES ON STAGE

A New Library

Review VOCABULARY

- community
- neighbors
- supermarket
- merchants
- business
- delivery
- energy
- reporter
- population
- tourists
- discover

CHARACTERS

Eduardo, 11 years old

Sofía, 10 years old, Eduardo's sister

Aunt Gracie, Eduardo and Sofía's aunt

Ms. Ming, furniture store owner

Mr. Jackson, supermarket owner

Mr. Perry, computer store owner

Narrator

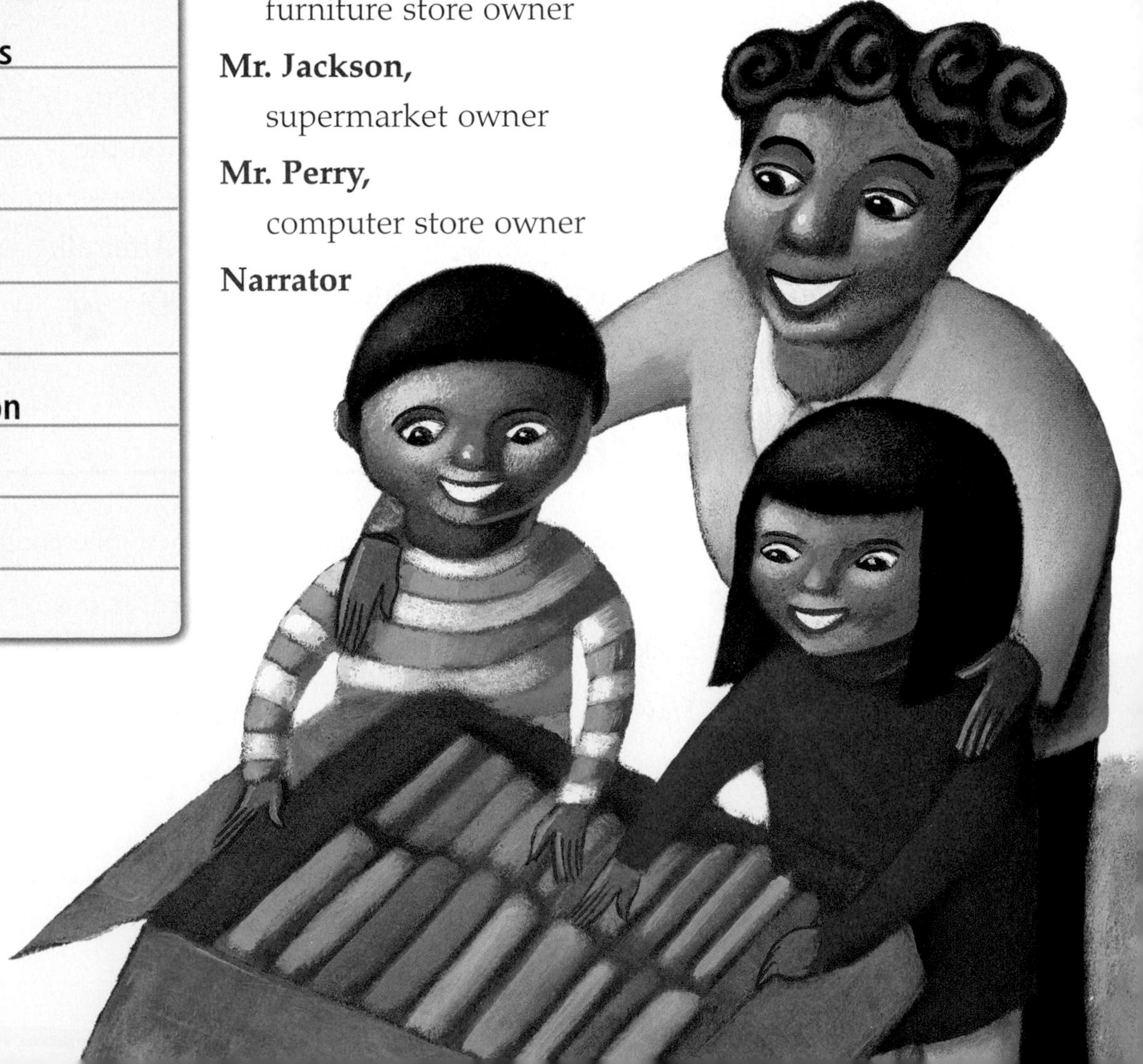

SCENE 1

SETTING: The basement of Aunt Gracie's house

Narrator: Sofía and Eduardo are helping Aunt Gracie clean out her basement.

Aunt Gracie: Eduardo, Sofía, thank you for helping me today.

Sofía: You're welcome, Aunt Gracie.

Eduardo: What's that big box in the corner?

Aunt Gracie: Let's see…

Narrator: Aunt Gracie opens the box.

Eduardo: Wow! Look at all those books!

Aunt Gracie: I've read every single one of them, but it would be a shame to throw them away.

Eduardo: Why don't we start a community library?

Aunt Gracie: What a good idea! The director of the Community Center is a friend of mine. I'm sure he'll let us use one of the rooms in the center as a library.

Sofía: A library needs tables and chairs.

Aunt Gracie: My neighbors, the Ming family, own a furniture store. I know Ms. Ming has some furniture that didn't get sold. Maybe she has some tables and chairs she could donate. Maybe some other people can help me, too.

Scene 2

SETTING: Ms. Ming's furniture store

Narrator: Eduardo, Sofía, and Aunt Gracie walk into Ms. Ming's furniture store.

Aunt Gracie: Hello, Ms. Ming. We were cleaning out my basement, and we found some old books. Eduardo suggested we start a community library.

Ms. Ming: That's a good idea. We could use a library.

Eduardo: Aunt Gracie says you have some furniture that you weren't able to sell. Do you have some tables and chairs we could use?

Ms. Ming: I sure do! I'd be happy to donate them to your library.

Sofía: Thanks, Ms. Ming!

SCENE 3

SETTING: Mr. Jackson's supermarket

Narrator: Aunt Gracie, Eduardo, and Sofía enter the
supermarket.

Mr. Jackson: Good morning! What can I do for you today?

Aunt Gracie: Good morning, Mr. Jackson. My niece and
nephew are planning to start a community library.

Mr. Jackson: That's a wonderful idea. How can I help?

Eduardo: We're asking local merchants and other business
people to donate materials. The library will need paper,
pencils, and pens.

Mr. Jackson: A supermarket sells more than food. We have
paper, pens, and pencils, too. I'd be happy to donate some
for the library. I even have some extra shelves I can give you.

Sofía: Great! We can use them to display the books. Thank you,
Mr. Jackson!

SCENE 4

SETTING: Mr. Perry's computer store

Narrator: Aunt Gracie, Eduardo, and Sofía enter the computer store.

Aunt Gracie: Good morning, Mr. Perry. We're going to start a community library soon.

Mr. Perry: That's fantastic! I'd like to help you with that.

Eduardo: Can you donate something from your business?

Mr. Perry: Yes! I can give you a computer. It's the old one I used for my business. I just bought a new computer, so I don't need the old one anymore.

Sofía: That would really help the library. Thank you, Mr. Perry.

Mr. Perry: You're welcome. Let me know when you need it, and I'll set up the delivery.

Scene 5

SETTING: The new library in the Community Center
Narrator: Aunt Gracie, Eduardo, and Sofía are in the library.

Eduardo: The library looks great! I'm glad you decided to volunteer as a librarian, Aunt Gracie.

Aunt Gracie: Well, it takes a lot of energy, but it's fun. The director of the Community Center told me he called a reporter from the *Brooksville Gazette* to write about the new library. He thinks it would make an interesting story.

Sofía: Soon the entire population of Brooksville will know about our library! We may even have tourists visiting us!

Aunt Gracie: The library was a wonderful idea, Eduardo. Just think of all the new things you'll discover in these books!

Eduardo: I may have come up with the idea, but it took everyone's help to make it happen.

307

Review Activities

Think and Respond

1. Compare two kinds of communities that you read about in this unit.

2. Did the colonists like the communities they lived in? How do you know?

3. Why do you think many Chinese immigrants chose to live in Chinatown?

4. If Grandpa had not received his community's support, do you think he would have closed his store? Why or why not?

5. How is an animal community similar to Lucy's neighborhood?

LANGUAGE STRUCTURE REVIEW

Talk About Possession

Form small groups. Place objects such as pens, pencils, or notebooks on your desk. Within your group, take turns pointing to different objects and asking one person to say who owns each object. Be sure to point to one of your own objects. Ask questions such as

- What color is Sara's backpack?
- Whose red pen is this?
  - What color is Alex's shirt?

1. Her backpack is blue and white.

2. That is my pen.

3. His shirt is green.

VOCABULARY REVIEW

Play "Five in a Row"

Form small groups with your classmates. Each group will need the Vocabulary Cards for the words in this unit. Each player will need a copy of a "Five in a Row" page. Use a pen to write twenty-five vocabulary words on the page. Write only one word in each box. Put the words in any order you like.

One group member chooses a Vocabulary Card and reads the word aloud. If you have that word on your page, use a pencil to make an X in the box. Continue until someone has five X's in a row. That person has to use each marked word in a sentence. He or she can call on classmates to think of some sentences. If the sentences are all correct, the person wins. The winner chooses the cards for the next round. Erase the marks on the page to play again.

space shuttle

astronaut

book

SING ALONG

Let's Explore

Let's fly through the universe,
universe, universe.
Let's fly through the universe,
To visit and explore.

We'll discover many things,
many things, many things.
We'll discover many things,
No one has seen before.

*Sing to the tune of
"Here We Go 'Round the Mulberry Bush."*

Draw Inferences

When you **draw inferences**, you use information in the text and illustrations and what you already know from experience to figure out what the author does not tell you.

Read the paragraph and question. Then look at the information in the chart to see how an inference was made.

Francesca looked at the train. Her hands were shaking. Her mother told her that many people enjoyed this new form of transportation because it was so much faster than traveling in a wagon. Francesca and her mother took their seats on the train, and it began to move.

How does Francesca feel about riding on the train?

Paragraph Information		My Experience		Inference
Francesca's hands are shaking.	**+**	Sometimes your hands shake when you're nervous or afraid.	**=**	Francesca is nervous about riding on the train.

Try This

▶ Read the paragraph and question. Then copy the chart and complete it, using the information from the paragraph.

Robert enjoyed learning about the solar system in science class and wanted to do well on the test. The test was difficult, but Robert had studied very hard. On Monday morning, Mrs. Velásquez handed back the tests. When Robert looked at his score, he smiled.

Did Robert do well on the test?

Paragraph Information		My Experience		Inference
	+		**=**	

Vocabulary POWER

From Here to There ▼

VOCABULARY

efficient

goods

transportation

building

waterways

travel

automobiles

exploration

Most people in the United States drive a car for **transportation**.

Ships were used for **exploration** of the world's oceans. Ships also carried **goods**, such as food or clothing, to different parts of the world.

An **automobile** like this old one uses a lot of gas.
It is not very **efficient**.

People use boats to **travel** along
waterways.

These construction workers are
building a new road.

From Here to There

People have always walked to get from one place to another. Walking, however, is not **efficient** for traveling great distances. It takes too long, and a walker cannot carry much. To get themselves and their **goods** where they need to go, people have had to use other forms of **transportation**.

The Wagon

covered wagon

In the 1700s and early 1800s, Americans mainly rode horses or used them to pull wagons, such as the Conestoga wagon. These covered wagons carried large, heavy loads over long distances. A team of four to six horses could pull a wagon that weighed as much as 6,000 pounds!

The Steamboat

While wagons were still being used, people were already building steamboats. These large, steam-powered boats quickly became an important way of moving people and goods on the country's rivers. Steamships, which are much larger than steamboats, could carry heavy loads across the Atlantic Ocean to other countries, such as England. A horse-drawn wagon couldn't do that!

train

The Railroad

In the 1800s, many Americans were moving west to areas without waterways. They couldn't take steamboats, and traveling by wagon was slow. The railroad made travel faster and easier. Trains carried people and goods faster than a wagon could, and crossing mountains was no longer a problem.

airplane

The Automobile

The railroad was efficient for traveling long distances, but people still had to use horses and wagons to go a mile or two. In the early 1900s, automobiles like Henry Ford's Model T made independent travel faster and easier. Cars are still our main form of transportation, but they have changed a lot since the Model T!

The Airplane

By the middle of the twentieth century, there were many ways to travel and to transport goods over long distances. The fastest was the airplane. A trip that takes only hours by airplane could take days by train. Imagine how long the same trip would have taken by wagon!

Model T automobile

space shuttle

The Space Shuttle

What is faster than an airplane? A space shuttle travels at about 17,500 miles per hour! Today we use shuttles for space exploration, not for everyday transportation. Maybe someday riding in a space shuttle will be as common as driving a car or flying in an airplane!

Related Vocabulary

Getting There

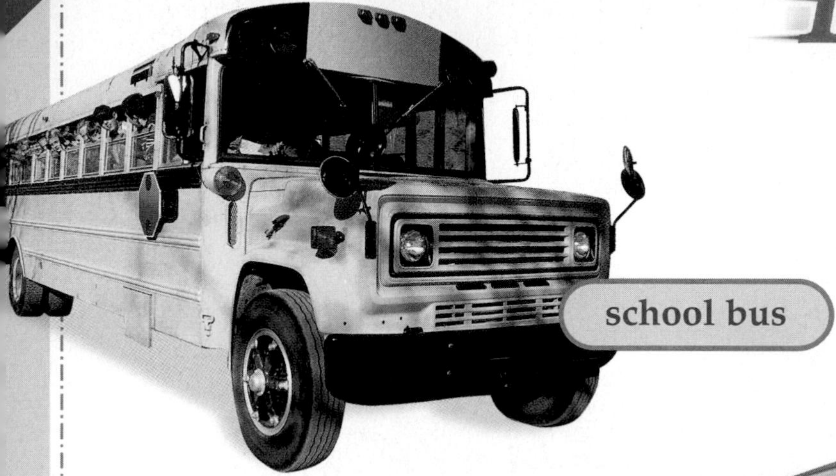
school bus

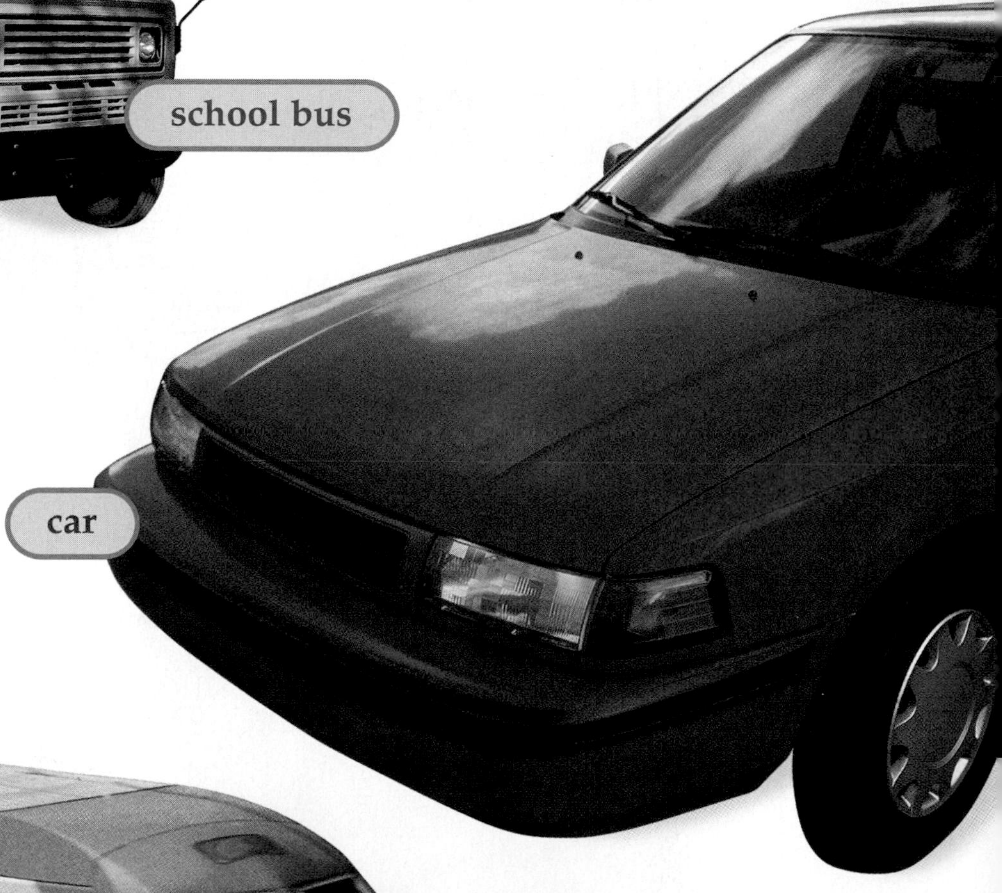
car

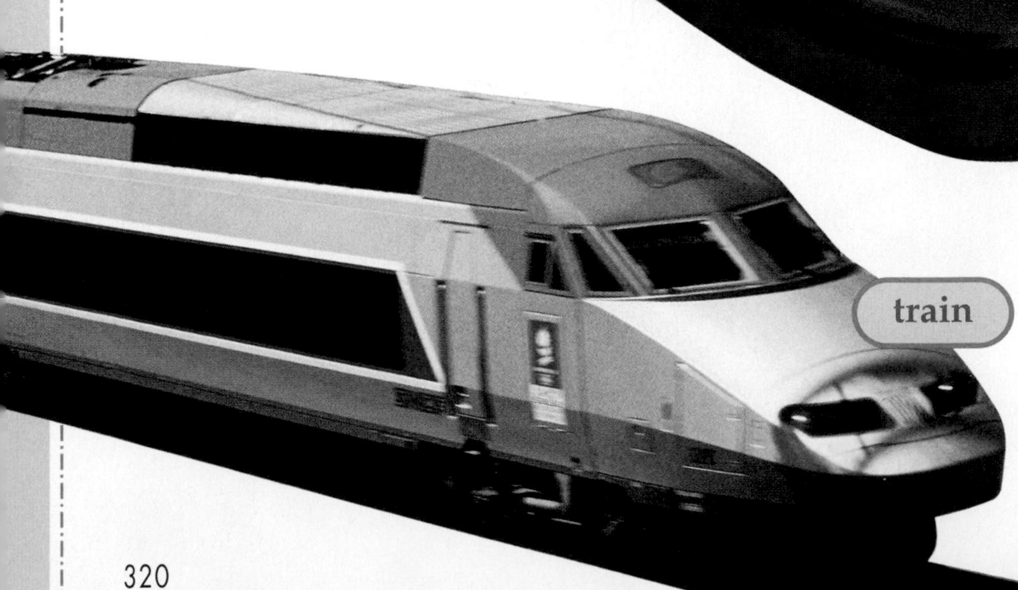
train

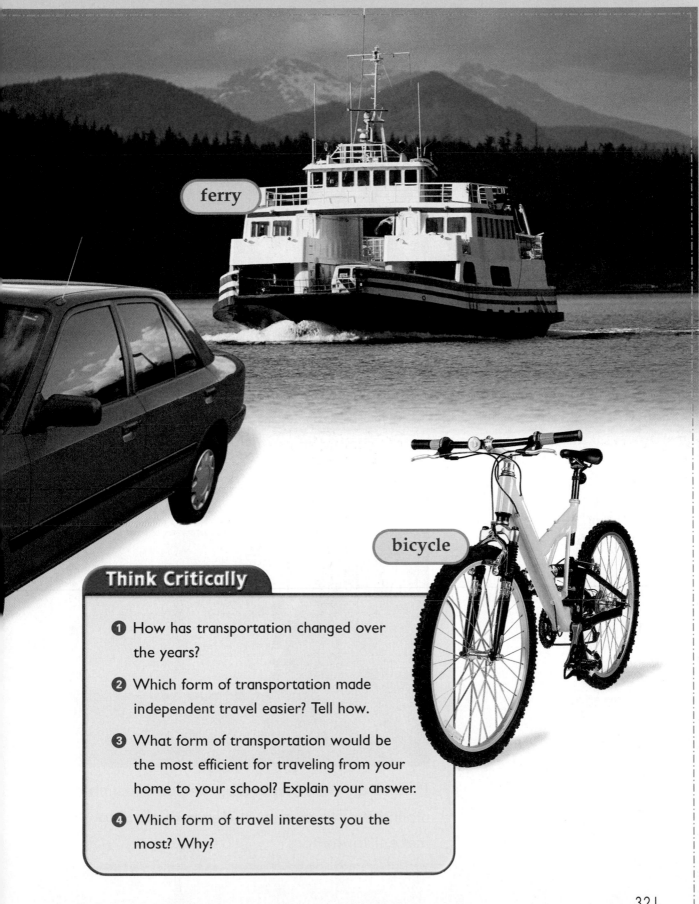

ferry

bicycle

Think Critically

1. How has transportation changed over the years?

2. Which form of transportation made independent travel easier? Tell how.

3. What form of transportation would be the most efficient for traveling from your home to your school? Explain your answer.

4. Which form of travel interests you the most? Why?

Vocabulary POWER

Amelia and Eleanor Go for a Ride ▼

VOCABULARY

determined

daring

speech

pilot

adventurous

independence

scarf

conversation

The flag of the United States is an important symbol of our nation's **independence**.

It takes an **adventurous** person to climb a mountain. This climber is **determined** to make it to the top.

When two or more people talk together, they have a **conversation**.

The **scarf** covered her head and neck.

This **daring** climber does not seem afraid of high places.

This **pilot** flies helicopters. On Career Day, he gave a **speech** about how he became a helicopter pilot.

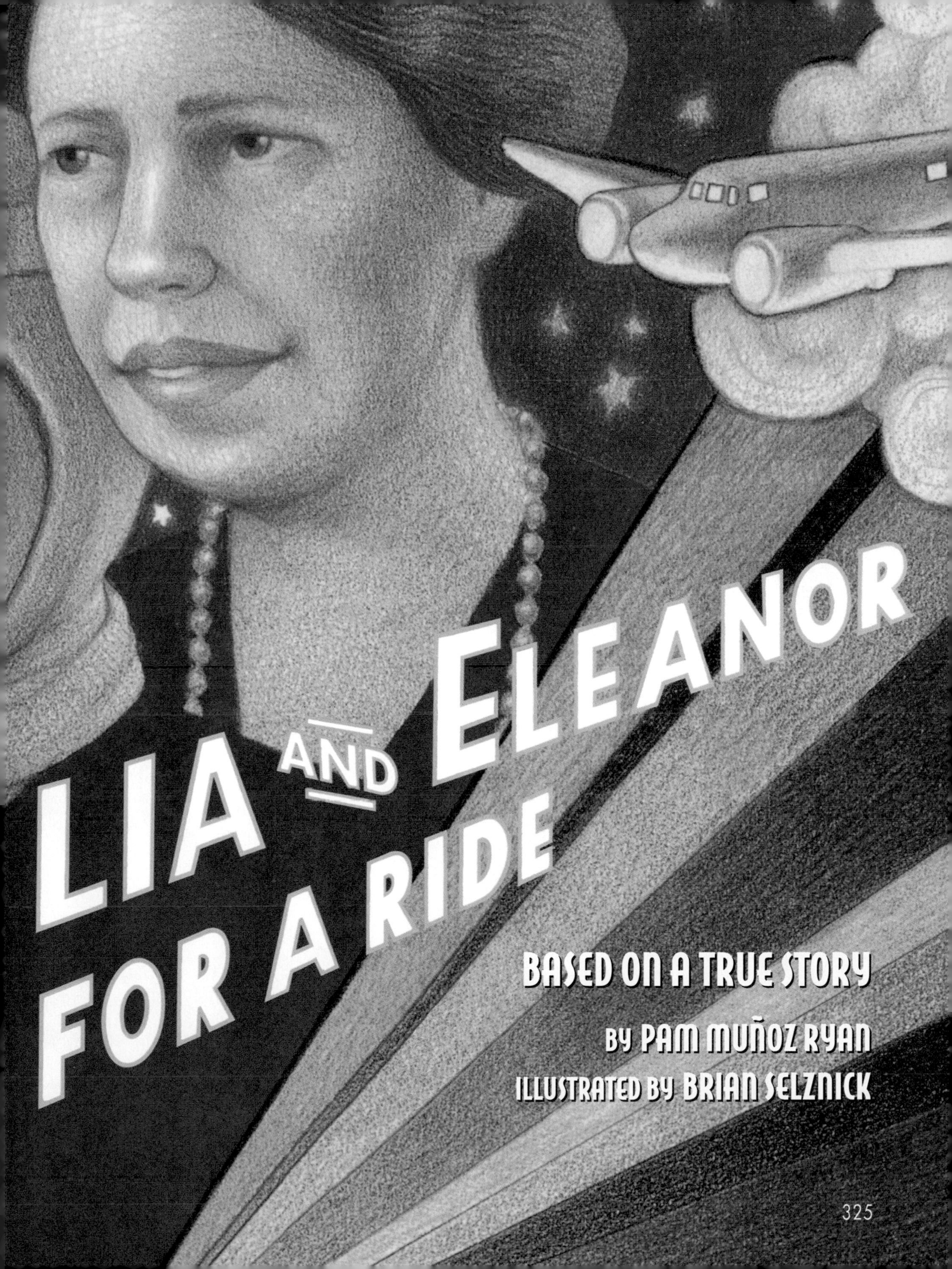

LIA AND ELEANOR FOR A RIDE

BASED ON A TRUE STORY

BY PAM MUÑOZ RYAN

ILLUSTRATED BY BRIAN SELZNICK

AMELIA AND ELEANOR were birds of a feather.
Eleanor was outspoken and determined.
So was Amelia.

Amelia was daring and liked to try things other women
wouldn't even consider.

Eleanor was the very same.

So when Eleanor discovered that her friend Amelia was
coming to town to give a speech, she naturally said, "Bring
your husband and come to dinner at my house! You can
even sleep over."

It wasn't unusual for two friends to get together. But
Eleanor was Eleanor Roosevelt, the First Lady of the United
States, who lived in the White House with her husband,
President Franklin Roosevelt.

Amelia was Amelia Earhart, the celebrated aviator who had been the first female pilot to fly solo across the Atlantic Ocean. And when two of the most famous and adventurous women in the world got together, something exciting was bound to happen.

In a guest room at the White House, Amelia and her husband, G.P., dressed for dinner. Amelia pulled on the long white evening gloves that were so different from the ones she sometimes wore while flying.

Many people didn't understand why a woman would want to risk her life in a plane. But Amelia had said it more than once: "It's for the fun of it." Besides, she loved the feeling of independence she had when she was in the cockpit.

She carefully folded a gift for Eleanor—a silk scarf that matched her own. The powder blue with streaks of indigo reminded Amelia of morning sky.

Meanwhile, Eleanor dressed for dinner, too. Her brother, Hall, would be escorting her this evening because the President had a meeting to attend. But Eleanor was used to that.

She pulled on the long white evening gloves that were so different from the ones she sometimes wore while driving. Then she peeked out the window at the brand-new car that had just been delivered that afternoon. She couldn't wait to drive it.

Many people thought it was too bold and dangerous for a woman to drive a car, especially the First Lady of the United States. But Eleanor always gave the same answer: "It's practical, that's all." Besides, she loved the feeling of independence she had when she was behind the wheel.

It was a brisk and cloudless April evening. The guests had gathered in the Red Room, and the table looked elegant, as even small dinner parties at the White House can be.

Eleanor and Hall greeted Amelia and G.P., as well as several reporters and a photographer.

Amelia gave Eleanor the scarf.

"I love it!" Eleanor exclaimed. "It's just like yours."

Dinner started with George Washington's crab chowder.

"This is delicious," said Amelia. "But if soup at the White House has such a fancy name, what will dessert be called?"

Perhaps Abraham Lincoln's peach cobbler? Or maybe

Thomas Jefferson's custard? They laughed as everyone took
turns guessing.

By the time they got to the roast duck, the conversation had
turned to flying.

"Mrs. Roosevelt just received her student pilot's license," said
one of the reporters.

Amelia wasn't surprised. She had been the one to encourage
Eleanor. She knew her friend could do anything she set her
mind to.

"I'll teach you myself," offered Amelia.

"I accept! Tell us, Amelia, what's it like to fly at night in the
dark?"

Everyone at the table leaned closer to hear. Very few
people in the whole world had ever flown at night, and
Amelia was one of them. Amelia's eyes sparkled. "The stars
glitter all about and seem close enough to touch.

"At higher elevations, the clouds below shine white with
dark islands where the night sea shows through. I've seen
the planet Venus setting on the horizon, and I've circled
cities of twinkling lights."

"And the capital city at night?" asked Eleanor.

"There's no describing it," said Amelia. "You just
have to experience it on a clear night, when you can see
forever. Why, we should go tonight! We could fly the loop
to Baltimore and back in no time!"

The Secret Service men protested. "This hasn't been
approved!"

"Nonsense!" said Eleanor. "If Amelia Earhart can fly
solo across the Atlantic Ocean, I can certainly take a short
flight to Baltimore and back!"

Before dessert could be served, Amelia had called
Eastern Air Transport and arranged a flight.

Within the hour, Amelia and Eleanor boarded the Curtis Condor twin-motor airplane. For a moment, both women looked up at the mysterious night sky. Then, without changing her gloves, Amelia slipped into the cockpit and took the wheel.

The plane rolled down the runway, faster and faster. Lights from the airstrip flashed in front of them. And they lifted into the dark.

"How amusing it is to see a girl in a white evening dress and high-heeled shoes flying a plane!" Eleanor said.

Amelia laughed as she made a wide sweep over Washington, D.C., and turned off all the lights in the plane.

Out the window, the Potomac River glistened with moonshine. The capitol dome reflected a soft golden halo. And the enormous, light-drenched monuments looked like tiny miniatures.

Soon the peaceful countryside gave way to shadowy woodlands. The Chesapeake Bay became a meandering outline on the horizon. And even though they knew it wasn't so, it seemed as if the plane crawled slowly through starstruck space.

Eleanor marveled, "It's like sitting on top of the world!"

When it was time to land, Amelia carefully took the
plane down. A group of reporters had gathered, anxious to
ask questions.

"Mrs. Roosevelt, did you feel safe knowing a girl was
flying that ship?"

"Just as safe!" said Eleanor.

"Did you fly the plane, Mrs. Roosevelt?" asked one
reporter.

"What part did you like best?" said another.

"I enjoyed it so much, and no, I didn't actually fly the
plane. Not yet. But someday I intend to. I was thrilled by the
city lights, the brilliance of the blinking pinpoints below."

Amelia smiled. She knew just how Eleanor felt.

As the Secret Service agents drove them slowly back
to the White House, Amelia and Eleanor agreed that
there was nothing quite as exciting as flying. What could
compare? Well, they admitted, maybe the closest thing
would be driving in a fast car on a straightaway road with
a stiff breeze blowing against your face.

Arms linked, they walked up the steps to the White House. Eleanor whispered something to Amelia, and then they hesitated, letting the rest of the group walk ahead of them.

"Are you coming inside, Mrs. Roosevelt?" someone asked.

But by then, they had wrapped their silk scarves around their necks and were hurrying toward Eleanor's new car.

Without changing her gloves, Eleanor quickly slipped into the driver's seat and took her turn at the wheel. With the wind in their hair and the brisk air stinging their cheeks, they flew down the road.

And after they had taken a ride about the city streets of Washington, D.C., they finally headed back to the White House . . . for dessert! Eleanor Roosevelt's pink clouds on angel food cake.

Think Critically

❶ Why was Amelia famous? Why was Eleanor famous?

❷ Was Amelia and Eleanor's friendship special? Explain.

❸ What was unusual about what Amelia and Eleanor did?

❹ If Amelia and Eleanor had invited you to go flying with them at night, would you have gone? Why or why not?

Vocabulary POWER

Journey Through the Solar System ▼

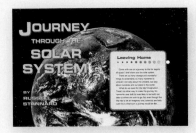

VOCABULARY

imagination

spaceship

Earth

Moon

horizon

gravity

distance

surface

astronauts

A **spaceship** of the future might look like this. The idea for this spaceship came from someone's **imagination**.

This is how the **Earth** looks from space.

338

The **Moon** is very far from Earth. It looks very small to us because of the great **distance**.

Walking on the **surface** of the Moon is different from walking on Earth. Since there is less **gravity** on the Moon, a person can jump very far.

Astronauts train for years to learn how to work safely in space.

The Earth appears to rise above the Moon's **horizon**.

JOURNEY

THROUGH THE

SOLAR

SYSTEM

BY
RUSSELL
STANNARD

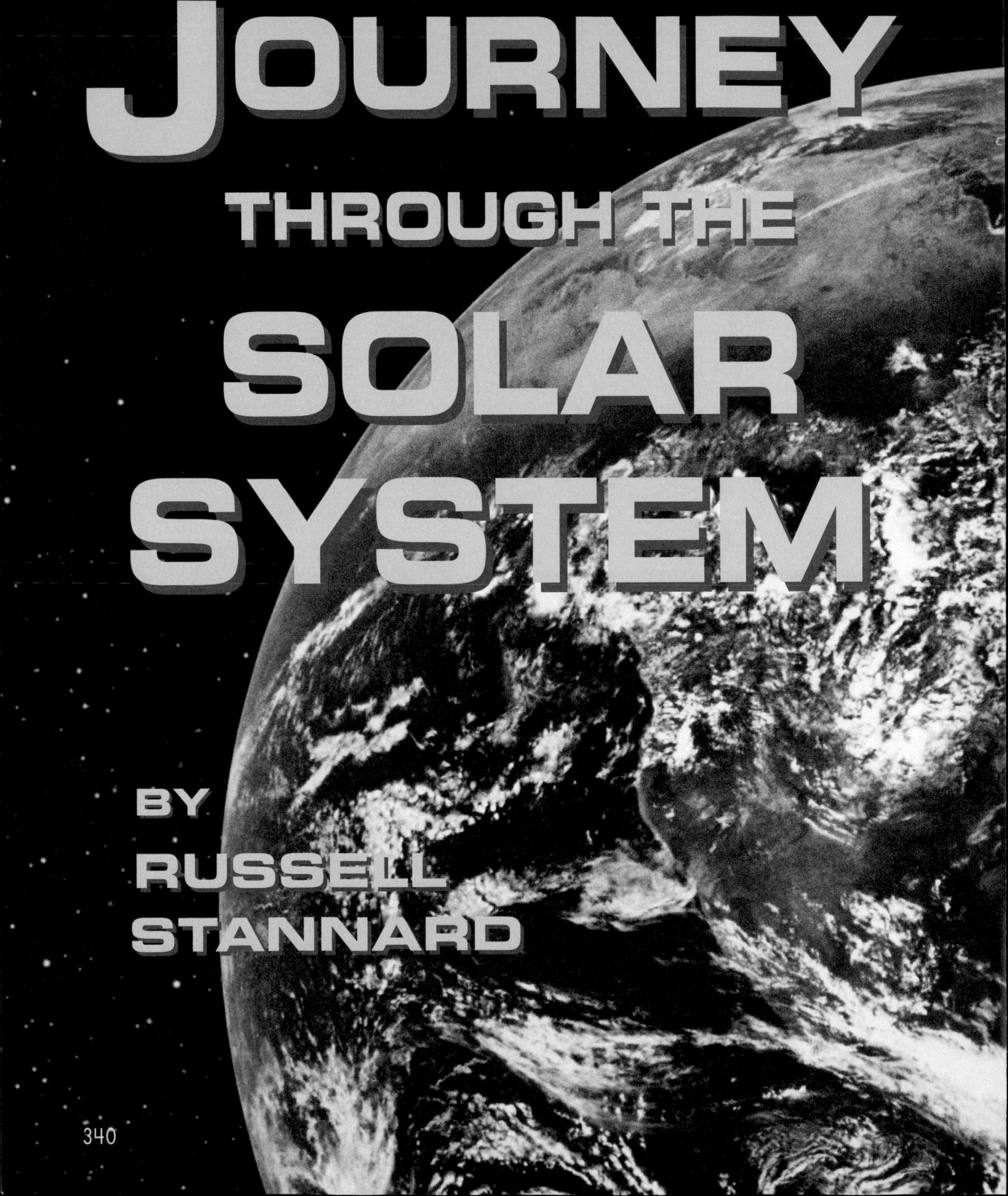

Leaving Home

Come with me on a journey to the far depths of space. I shall show you the solar system.

There are so many strange and wonderful things to understand, so many mysteries to unravel—not only about the universe, but also about ourselves and our place in the world.

What do we need for the trip? Imagination. There's no other way to make this journey. No spaceship ever built (or ever likely to be built) can take us where we wish to go. But even though the trip has to be an imaginary one, scientists are fairly sure this is what such a journey would be like . . .

Just a Minute!

Before we blast off into space, let's think for a moment. The Earth we live on is part of the universe we wish to explore. Except for the Moon, and possibly the nearby planets, it is the only part of the universe we can actually get our hands on. The laws of nature that rule everything going on here might be the same laws that apply everywhere else. So why not take a quick look around here on Earth, before we launch out into the unknown?

Round or Flat?

First of all, there is the shape of the Earth. Long ago, everyone thought the Earth was flat—apart from the odd hill or valley, of course. There's no doubt it looks flat. At the seaside the water seems to stretch on forever, as far as the eye can see.

But suppose on a clear day we look through a pair of binoculars at a distant ship. As it travels away from us, it seems to sink as it disappears over the horizon.

This is because the Earth is actually round. It is a ball 7,926 miles (12,756 km) across.

Going Down

Right under our feet, nearly 8,000 miles (13,000 km) down, is the other side of the Earth. What keeps the people who live there from falling off?

First we have to stop thinking that there is some special direction in space called "down," such that everything is pulled in that direction. All directions in space are similar to one another. The important thing is that when something falls, it falls toward the Earth—it is the Earth that does the pulling.

To do this, our planet uses a force, an invisible one, called gravity. The strength of this force depends on how far away you are from the Earth. The bigger the distance, the weaker the force. If you go twice the distance away from the Earth's center, the force drops to a quarter; three times the distance, a ninth; ten times the distance, a hundredth; and so on. But although it gets weaker and weaker, it never completely disappears; it stretches out into space, to infinity.

The force is strongest on the surface of the Earth. Gravity is what holds you down in your seat at this very moment. If you get up and jump, gravity will pull you back again.

Although the Earth is round, it's not a perfect sphere—it bulges slightly at the equator. The diameter through the center of the Earth is 7,900 miles from pole to pole, but 7,926 miles across the equator.

Now, if you and I are pulled toward the center of the Earth, the same will be true of everyone else, wherever they are on the surface of the Earth. They will all talk about being pulled "down." But all their "downs" are different.

The Force That Shapes the Universe

It is not just the things outside the Earth that feel the pull of gravity; the stuff that makes up the Earth itself feels it too. Every part of the Earth is pulling on every other part of it. That's why the Earth ends up round; it's the best way of packing things

"How come people on the other side of the world don't fall off?"

"How come people on the other side of the world don't fall off?"

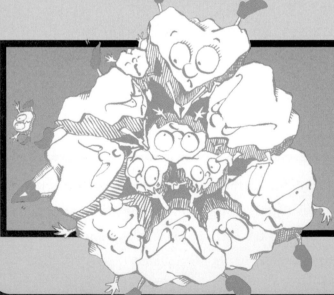

Gravity makes every part of the Earth pull on every other part and tries to drag them all to the center. That's why our planet is round.

together so that they can all get as close as possible to one another. All the bits of rock and dirt try to get to the center of the Earth, but they are stopped by others that got there first.

Why am I telling you this? The point is, even before we get in our rocket and leave the Earth, we already have some idea of what we are likely to find out on our travels. If the Earth attracts everything with gravity, then perhaps everything we'll come across in space attracts everything else with gravity. In fact, we shall find *it is the force of gravity that shapes the entire universe.* Not only that, but if being round is the most practical shape for the Earth, then most things out there are likely to be round too.

Looking Up

When we look up at the sky, to where we shall soon be heading, what do we see? The Sun, the Moon, and the stars. They are all moving slowly across the sky and around our planet. Or are they? They certainly appear to be. But people have been fooled by appearances before. Learning things often involves unlearning things first. (Remember the "down" that wasn't everyone's "down.")

For example, people used to think the sky was a great hollow dome, with twinkly lights (the stars) stuck to it. They were amazed to learn that it wasn't so. Not only that, but the stars, the Sun, and the Moon were not going around the Earth once every 24 hours. It was the Earth that was spinning. The Earth completes one of its turns every 24-hour day.

When people still believed everything went around the Earth, we thought we were at the center of the universe. That meant we human beings must be very important. We *are* important (at least, I think so), but not for that reason. This is an example of the way discoveries about the universe can raise interesting questions about ourselves.

The fact that the Earth spins like a top leads us to expect that most other things we shall discover in our travels will also be spinning.

Where To?

The largest objects in the sky are, of course, the Sun and Moon. They appear to be roughly the same size. But again we must be careful. The apparent size of something depends on how far away it is.

In fact, the Moon is much closer. It is our nearest neighbor in space. So it sounds like a good place, at long last, to start our space journey.

The Moon is almost 400 times closer to the Earth than the Sun is, and 100 times closer than the nearest planet.

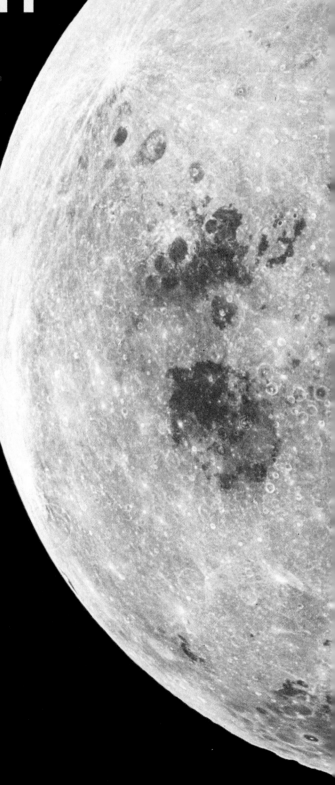

First Stop: The Moon

Three . . . two . . . one . . . blast off!

As we approach the Moon, the first thing we notice is that it is a round ball; it is not a flat disk, which is what it looks like from Earth. (But a round ball is the shape we expect from gravity, right?)

Secondly, the Man in the Moon has disappeared! His face, with those staring eyes and the open mouth which always seems to be saying "Oooh," has broken up into mountains and valleys pitted with deep holes and craters. These were made by meteoroids, thousands of rocks that fly through space and crash into anything that gets in their way.

Unlike the meteoroids, we land our craft gently.

The Moon's diameter is 2,160 mi. (3,476 km). That is roughly equal to the distance across Australia. It would take 81 Moons to weigh the same as Earth.

Twelve astronauts walked on the Moon between 1969 and 1972. Their footprints are still there, in the moondust that covers the surface. This is because there is no wind and rain to wear them away.

Going for a Stroll

Walking on the Moon is fun. You feel very light. You can take big, big steps. And boy how you can jump! Six times as high as on the Earth.

This is because the Moon's gravity force is not as strong as the Earth's—only one-sixth. Your weight depends on the gravity force. If gravity is only one-sixth as strong, your weight on the Moon will be only one-sixth of your weight on the Earth.

Why is the Moon's gravity so much less than the Earth's? The Moon does not have as much mass as the Earth; it is not as heavy. In the first place, it is smaller. In the second, the material from which it is made has a lower density; it is not packed together as tightly as the Earth's material.

But although the Moon's gravity is weak, notice that *it does have a gravity force*. (Don't be fooled by those pictures of astronauts floating around weightless inside their spacecraft.) Remember, *everything* has a gravity force.

Give Me Air!

Because the Moon's gravity is so weak, there is no atmosphere here; the Moon can't hold on to one. The atmosphere, if there ever was one, just floated away. There is no air, no water, no life—all very different from the Earth.

This is why astronauts must wear space suits on the Moon; they have to carry their own supply of air to breathe.

The Far Side

Just as the Earth spins around like a top as it orbits the Sun, so the Moon spins too. It takes 27.3 days, roughly one month, to spin around once, which is the same time it takes to orbit the Earth. And that means we always see the same side of the Moon on Earth. We call this side the near side. Until a spacecraft sent back photographs in 1959, no one had ever seen the far side. What did the photos show? Oddly, many many more craters than on the near side.

And now we must leave the Moon. "Already?" you ask. I'm afraid so. Quite frankly, our travels have much more exciting things in store!

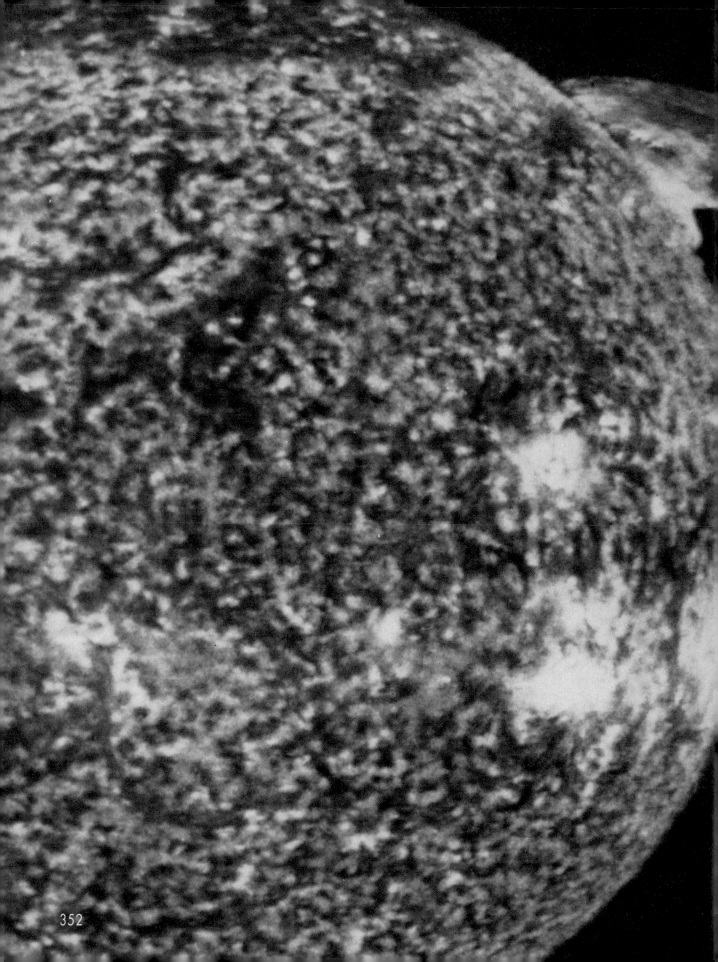

THE SUN:
A Bomb That Goes Off Slowly

As seen from the Earth, the Moon and the Sun may look similar. In fact, they are very different. The Moon is a round dusty rock; the Sun is a huge ball of flaming hot gas. And I do mean huge; the distance from one side of the Sun to the other, its diameter, is 865,000 miles (1.4 million km). That is 109 times the diameter of the Earth. The reason it doesn't look a lot bigger than the Moon is that the Sun is much farther away.

Because the Sun's gas is so hot, it swirls and rushes and jiggles around a lot. You might think that all this movement would throw the gas off into space.

More than one million Earths could fit inside the Sun.

But no. The Sun has 333,000 times the mass of the Earth, and it has an *enormous* gravity force. It is this force that keeps the gas together.

Next Stop, the Sun?

take-off ...

Just as the Moon orbits the Earth, so the Earth orbits the Sun. It does this once every 365 days—in other words, once a year. And it stays at a distance of roughly 93 million miles (150 million km) from the Sun. That is a long way. A spacecraft traveling at the speed of a jumbo jet would take about 20 years to get to the Sun. (That's a lot of inflight movies!) If, like an airplane flight, the fare was based on a rate of about 18 cents per mile, a one-way ticket would cost nearly $17 million!

As you approach the Sun (but not too closely!), you'll see that its surface is anything but smooth and regular. The flaming hot gas is always seething and swirling about. Some of the gas leaps up high; these are called solar prominences. The surface is also marked by darker patches known as sunspots; these are regions of somewhat cooler gas.

...arrival

Spring, Summer, Fall, Winter

The Earth's orbit around the Sun is almost a circle, but not quite. It is slightly squashed. We call its oval shape an ellipse. So our distance from the Sun varies slightly during the year it takes us to complete the orbit. Is this why we have hot weather in summer and cold in winter?

No. The effect of this varying distance is very tiny. The real reason for the different seasons has to do with the way the Earth spins while it is orbiting the Sun. As we have already learned, the Earth spins like a top. It does this around an imaginary line that joins the North and South poles and is called the axis.

Looking at the diagram, you can see how this North-South axis is tilted to one side. Suppose it was *not* like this. Suppose it was bolt upright. Then there would be no seasons; the weather would stay the same all year round. The only effect of spinning would be to give us night and day—night when we were facing away from the Sun, day when we faced toward it.

But that is not how the axis is arranged. It is tilted. So, if we live in the North, at one stage of the orbit the axis tends to tip us slightly toward the Sun—the Sun beats down on us and we get long, hot summer days. Meanwhile, those living in the South are pointed away from the Sun; its rays hit them at only a glancing angle, and that's when they get their winter. On the opposite side of the orbit, six months later, we change places; it is then our turn to have winter, and theirs to have summer.

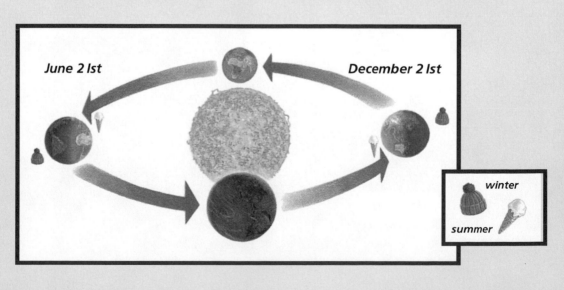

June 2 lst   *December 2 lst*

winter

summer

Related Vocabulary

THE SOLAR SYSTEM

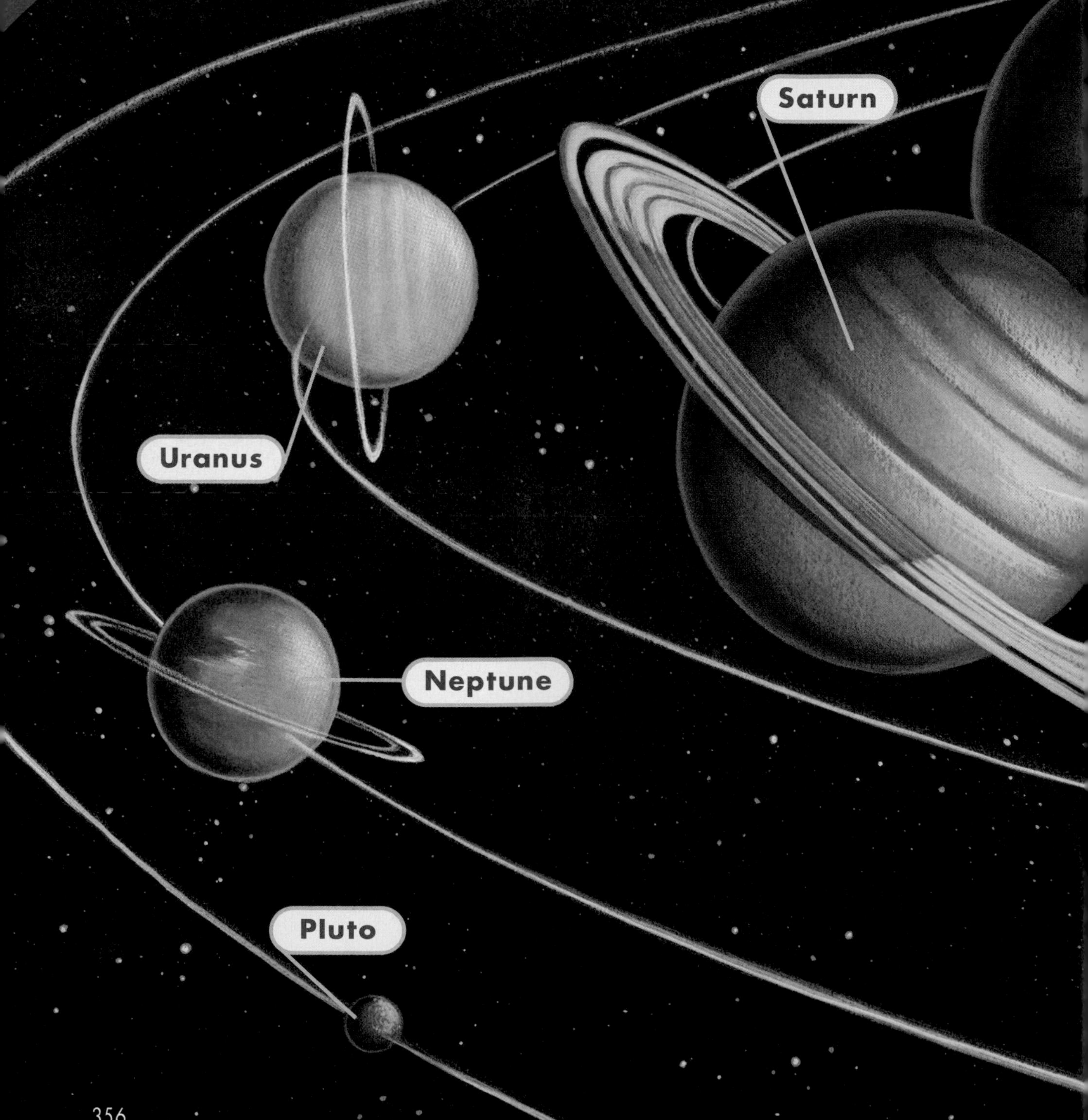
Saturn
Uranus
Neptune
Pluto

Sun

Jupiter

Earth

Venus

Mercury

Mars

Think Critically

1 In what ways are the Earth and the Moon alike? How are they different?

2 Why do the Sun and the Moon appear to be the same size?

3 Is it possible to land on the Sun? How do you know?

4 What did you learn about the solar system that you did not know before?

Vocabulary POWER

Letters from Space ▼

VOCABULARY

flight

nutritious

vacation

controls

dunes

laboratory

interesting

exercise

This summer my family took a **vacation** to Florida. Our **flight** arrived just before sunset.

Fish and vegetables are **nutritious** foods. They contain vitamins and minerals that are good for the body.

The pilot **controls** the airplane from the cockpit. That job seems very **interesting**.

Bicycling, walking, and jogging are all forms of **exercise**.

This scientist performs her experiments in a **laboratory**.

In this desert, there are sand **dunes** as far as the eye can see.

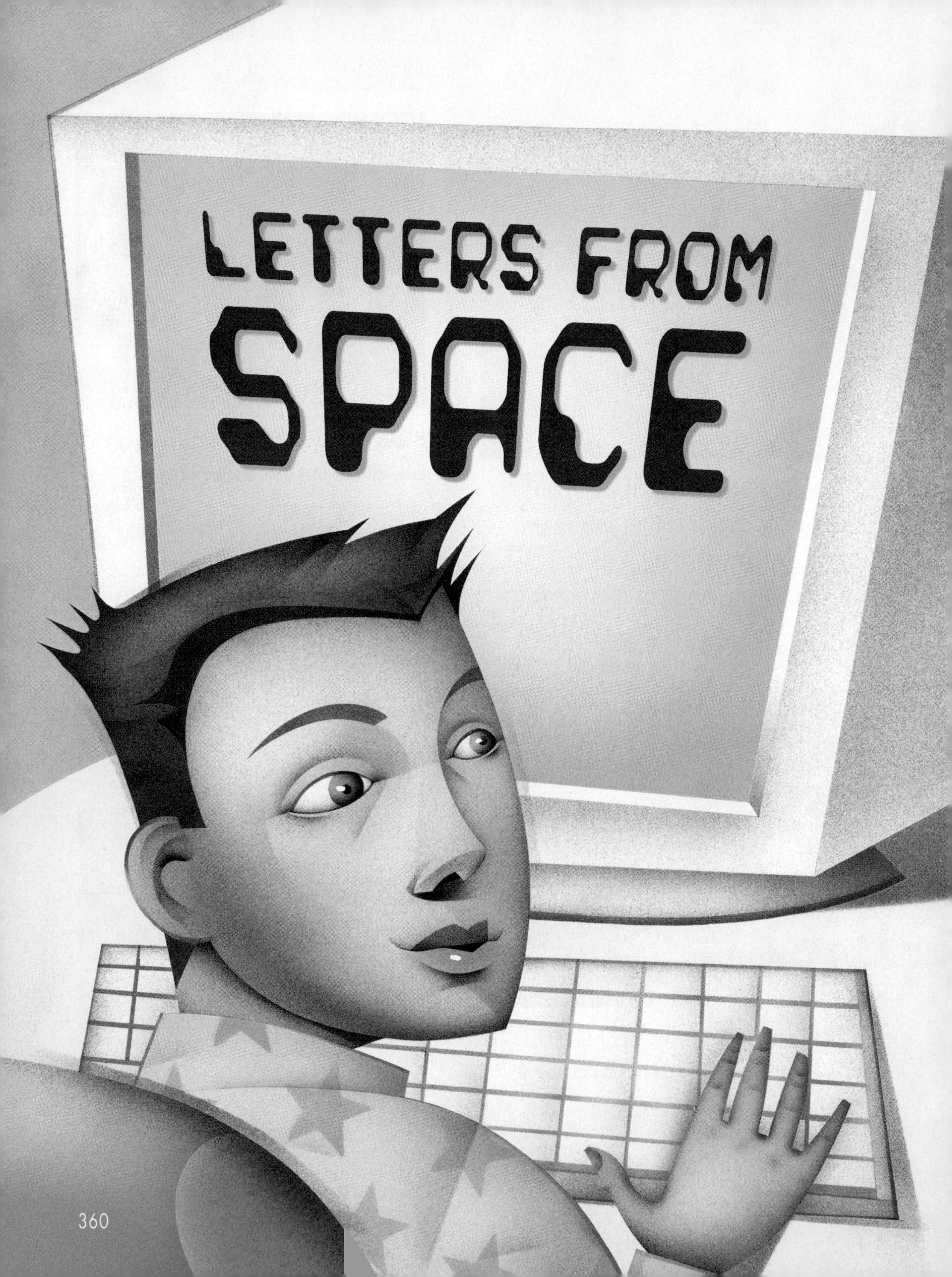
LETTERS FROM
SPACE

Dear John,

We've finally arrived on Mars! The flight took all day, but the trip was so much fun! I saw the brightest lights and most beautiful sky you can imagine. The food on the flight was very different from what we normally eat. All of our food was served in small foil packets. My mother said it was nutritious, but it wasn't as good as the food she cooks.

We'll be here until December because my father has a lot of work to do at his job. Everyone I've met is really friendly, and I've learned a little bit about how things work here.

I already miss you and all of our friends, but I think I will make friends here. At least I have my own room and a computer, just like at home. I promise to write often while I'm here.

Your friend,
Ana

Dear Ana,

It was great hearing from you! School is over, and the sunny summer days are here. How does the sun look from there? I imagine it must look different from the way we see it on Earth.

My parents have decided that I'm old enough to cut the grass. I guess there isn't any grass where you are. Lucky for you!

I'm excited about my vacation. This summer we're going camping in the Grand Canyon. My little sister wanted to go to the beach, but I think she'll enjoy camping.

What does the land on Mars look like? Are there mountains, forests, and beaches like the ones here?

Your Earth friend,
John

AUGUST 15, 2035

Dear John,

Even though it's summer here too, we don't go outside. We can't breathe the air, and it's very cold because the sun is farther from Mars than it is from Earth. My house and yard are covered by a big glass dome. A computer controls the temperature and the oxygen level inside. We do have grass here, inside the dome. Like you, I have to cut it! Under the dome we also grow flowers, vegetables, and even some trees. It's almost like home. From my bedroom window I can see a beautiful red desert, with dunes and rocks in strange shapes. I think our desert looks like the land around the Grand Canyon.

I made a new friend named Natasha. She's from Russia, and she's been here for six months. We have a lot of fun together. Sometimes we visit the laboratory where our parents work. They're designing systems to bring water to the desert so that more people will want to come here. Maybe someday you'll come here and see all the amazing things for yourself.

Your friend,
Ana

Dear Ana,

We went back to school this week, and everyone asked about you. We're studying some interesting new subjects in sixth grade. My favorite subject is science. I told my teacher that I want to work in a laboratory one day.

I'm busy with school and homework, but I still have time for fun. I'm on the school's baseball team, and I hit a home run in yesterday's game! I wish you could've seen it.

Only three months are left until you come home! Everyone at school wants to hear about your trip. They're amazed that you live inside a dome! I hope you're taking lots of pictures.

Your baseball star,
John

Dear John,

I started school, too. We're learning a lot about computers. We also study math, reading, and social studies, just as we did back home. One thing that's really different here is gym class. Since we can't go outside, there's a big gym where we all go to exercise. I like to ride the stationary bikes. Natasha and I choose bikes next to each other so we can talk as we pedal. That makes exercising more fun.

The students here come from all over the world, and I've made a lot of friends. We spend time together after school, watching movies or doing our homework. Even though life here is different and exciting, I miss my friends back home, especially you. I won't be here much longer, though. Soon I'll be able to see you again.

Take care!
Ana

Dear Ana,

There's only one month now until you come back! I haven't changed much since you left. I'm a little bit taller, and my hair is longer. When you come home, we can play baseball together, if it hasn't snowed by then. My mom said she'll take us for pizza! Doesn't that sound like a great welcome home? I hope you have a good flight back to Earth.

Your friend,
John

DECEMBER 17, 2035

Dear John,

I'm finally coming home! I had a great time here. I made some good friends, learned a lot, and saw things I'd never seen before. I know that someday I'll come back to visit, but I'm very happy to be going home. Soon I'll look up at the sky on Earth, and I'll see the bright red light that is Mars—an interesting planet, and now my second home.

See you soon!
Ana

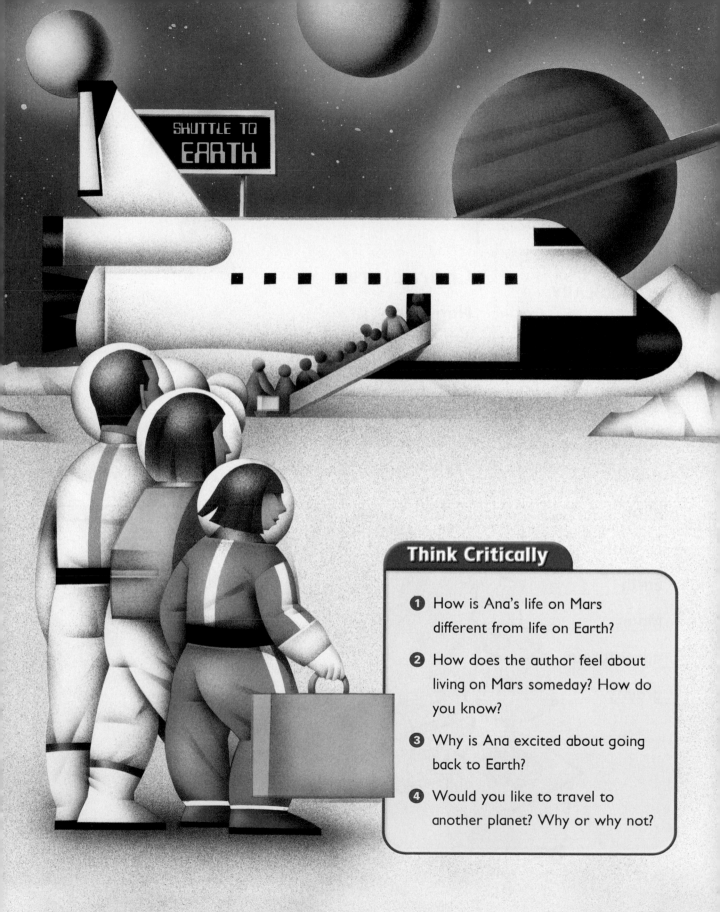

Think Critically

1. How is Ana's life on Mars different from life on Earth?

2. How does the author feel about living on Mars someday? How do you know?

3. Why is Ana excited about going back to Earth?

4. Would you like to travel to another planet? Why or why not?

Review Vocabulary with a Play

STORIES ON STAGE

A Space Emergency

Review
VOCABULARY

astronaut

exploration

determined

interesting

travel

pilot

controls

Earth

Moon

adventurous

gravity

Characters

Narrator
Juan González, *10 years old*
Mrs. González, *Juan's mother*
Astronaut Adams, *main astronaut*
Astronaut Jones, *pilot*
Mr. Ling, *teacher*
Students

Scene 1

SETTING: Juan's bedroom

Narrator: Mrs. González walks into Juan's bedroom.

Mrs. González: Juan! Juan! Wake up. It's time to get ready for school.

Juan: I'm tired, Mom.

Mrs. González: Your class is taking a field trip today! You're going to the Space Center, remember?

Juan *(sitting up)*: Oh, yes! I forgot. Our teacher said we're going to meet Astronaut Adams.

Mrs. González: I've heard about Astronaut Adams. She's done a lot of space exploration.

Juan: Yes. I want to be an astronaut like her when I grow up. Being an astronaut must be exciting!

Mrs. González: Being an astronaut is also hard work, Juan. You have to study hard and be very determined. Now hurry up, or you'll miss the bus.

369

Scene 2

SETTING: The Space Center

Mr. Ling: Class, this is Astronaut Adams. She has something interesting to tell us.

Students: Hello, Astronaut Adams!

Astronaut Adams: Hello, students. Today I'll travel into space to fix a broken satellite.

Students: Wow!

Astronaut Adams: I need a student volunteer to travel with me. You see, I can't fit inside the satellite to fix it.

Narrator: Juan raises his hand.

Juan: I'd like to volunteer. I'm Juan, and I want to be an astronaut.

Astronaut Adams: I think you'll make a fine astronaut, Juan. Come with me.

Mr. Ling: Have a nice trip, Juan!

Scene 3

SETTING: Inside the space shuttle

Astronaut Adams: Juan, this is Astronaut Jones. He's the pilot of the space shuttle.

Juan: Hello, Astronaut Jones. There are a lot of buttons here. Do you know what each one does?

Astronaut Jones: Of course—that's my job. Each one controls part of the space shuttle.

Astronaut Adams: We're ready for takeoff, Juan. Put on your seat belt and prepare for the adventure of your life!

Astronaut Jones: Five, four, three, two, one!

Narrator: Everything shakes as the space shuttle takes off.

Juan: Look! You can see the Earth.

Astronaut Jones *(pointing)*: Look out this window. The Moon is shining brightly over there.

Juan: Everything looks so small now. This is quite a view!

Astronaut Adams: Are you feeling adventurous, Juan? There's the satellite!

Juan: How can we go outside? Won't we fall?

Astronaut Adams: Gravity is making us fall right now. We're also moving forward very fast. Those two movements keep us moving in a circle around the Earth. Also, we'll be connected to the space shuttle by our air hoses.

Narrator: Astronaut Adams and Juan exit the shuttle and climb onto the satellite.

Juan: This isn't so easy.

Astronaut Adams: Juan! Your air hose is caught in the satellite's door!

Juan: Oh, no! I'm stuck! Help!

Scene 4

SETTING: Juan's bedroom

Narrator: Juan is in bed, caught in his blanket. He is trying to pull it off.

Juan: Oh, no! I'm stuck! Help!

Mrs. González *(shaking Juan)*: Wake up, Juan! Wake up!

Juan *(waking up and looking around)*: What? What happened? Where am I?

Mrs. González: You're in bed.

Juan: In bed? No, I was outside the space shuttle fixing a satellite in space.

Mrs. González: Fixing a satellite in space? That was a dream!

Juan: Oh! Now I remember that our class has a field trip today. We're going to the Space Center.

Mrs. González: That's right. You'll learn many interesting things there.

Juan: Well, I already learned one thing. Being an astronaut is hard work!

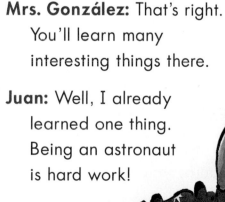

Review Activities

Think and Respond

1 What are some of the forms of transportation you read about in this unit? Which ones have you used?

2 How have the ways that people explore changed over time?

3 Compare and contrast traveling by airplane with traveling by train.

4 What are some of the things that scientists have learned about the Earth and the Moon?

5 Why do you think people want to explore space?

LANGUAGE STRUCTURE REVIEW

Predict Future Events

Use these sentence beginnings to write three sentences that predict future events.
• If a person studies hard for a test,...
• If the weather is warm over the weekend,...
• If people continue to explore new places,...

Then form small groups with your classmates. Take turns reading your sentences. Talk about what might happen in the future.

1. If a person studies hard for a test, he or she can do well on the test.

2. If the weather is warm over the weekend, we can play baseball.

3. If people continue to explore new places, they will learn new things.

VOCABULARY REVIEW

Act It Out!

Form small groups with your classmates. Each person in a group must choose a Vocabulary Card. Work together with your group to plan a short skit. As your group performs the skit, each person should hold up the Vocabulary Card when he or she uses the word. Each word should be used at least once.

transportation

adventurous

imagination

interesting

Using the Glossary

A glossary is like a dictionary. It lists words in alphabetical order. To find a word, look it up by its first letter or letters.

To save time, use the guide words. They are at the top of each page. They tell you the first and last entry words on the page. Look at the guide words to see if your word comes between them in the alphabet.

Here is an example of a glossary entry:

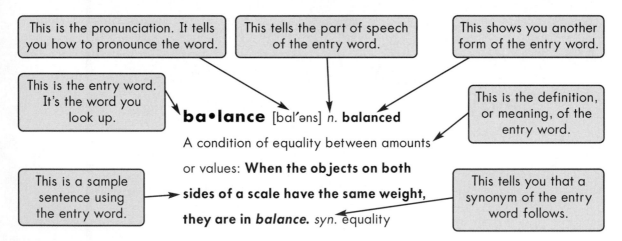

This is the pronunciation. It tells you how to pronounce the word.

This tells the part of speech of the entry word.

This shows you another form of the entry word.

This is the entry word. It's the word you look up.

This is the definition, or meaning, of the entry word.

ba•lance [bal′əns] *n.* **balanced**
A condition of equality between amounts or values: **When the objects on both sides of a scale have the same weight, they are in *balance.*** *syn.* equality

This is a sample sentence using the entry word.

This tells you that a synonym of the entry word follows.

Word Origins

Sometimes an entry word is followed by a note about the word's origin, or beginning. The note tells you how the word began and how it has changed over time. Words often have interesting backgrounds that can help you remember what they mean.

Here is an example of a word origin note:

fraction The word *fraction* comes from the Latin verb *frangere,* meaning "to break." Fractions name the parts of objects or groups that have been "broken" into equal parts.

Pronunciation

The pronunciation is in brackets that look like this [ ]. It is a respelling of the entry word, and it shows how the word is pronounced.

This **pronunciation key** tells you what the symbols in a respelling mean.

Pronunciation Key*

a	add, map	m	move, seem	u	up, done		
ā	ace, rate	n	nice, tin	û(r)	burn, term		
â(r)	care, air	ng	ring, song	yōō	fuse, few		
ä	palm, father	o	odd, hot	v	vain, eve		
b	bat, rub	ō	open, so	w	win, away		
ch	check, catch	ô	order, jaw	y	yet, yearn		
d	dog, rod	oi	oil, boy	z	zest, muse		
e	end, pet	ou	pout, now	zh	vision, pleasure		
ē	equal, tree	ŏŏ	took, full	ə	the schwa, an		
f	fit, half	ōō	pool, food		unstressed vowel		
g	go, log	p	pit, stop		representing the		
h	hope, hate	r	run, poor		sound spelled		
i	it, give	s	see, pass		*a* in *above*		
ī	ice, write	sh	sure, rush		*e* in *sicken*		
j	joy, ledge	t	talk, sit		*i* in *possible*		
k	cool, take	th	thin, both		*o* in *melon*		
l	look, rule	th	this, bathe		*u* in *circus*		

Other symbols
• separates words into syllables
´ indicates heavier stress on a syllable
´ indicates light stress on a syllable

Abbreviations: *adj.* adjective, *adv.* adverb, *conj.* conjunction, *interj.* interjection, *n.* noun, *prep.* preposition, *pron.* pronoun, *syn.* synonym, *v.* verb

*The Pronunciation Key and adapted entries are reprinted from *HBJ School Dictionary*. Copyright © 1990 by Harcourt, Inc. Reprinted by permission of Harcourt, Inc.

ad•ven•tur•ous [ad•ven′chər•əs] *adj.* Liking unusual, thrilling, or risky experiences: **Columbus was an *adventurous* sailor.** *syn.* daring

air•port [âr′pôrt′] *n.* A large area set up for the landing and taking off of aircraft and for the loading and unloading of passengers and freight: **The airplane landed at the *airport*.** *syn.* airfield

a•lone [ə•lōn′] *adv.* Without anyone else present or helping: **Chen does his homework *alone*.**

an•ces•tor [an′ses′tər] *n.* **an•ces•tors** A person from whom one is descended, generally a person further back than a grandparent: **This picture of my *ancestors* was taken 100 years ago.**

a•part•ment [ə•pärt′mənt] *n.* A group of rooms, or a single room, to live in: **My brother's *apartment* has three bedrooms.**

as•tro•naut [as′trə•nôt′] *n.* **as•tro•nauts** A person who travels in space: ***Astronauts* must have a lot of training before they go into space.**

astronaut

Word Origins
astronaut The word *astronaut* was formed by combining two Greek word parts: *astro*, meaning "star," and *nautes*, meaning "sailor." An astronaut is a "sailor of the stars"!

ath•lete [ath′lēt′] *n.* A person with skill in sports or games such as football, running, or tennis: **I think Marcy is the best *athlete* on the team.**

athletes

au•to•mo•bile [ô′tə•mə•bēl′] *n.* **au•to•mo•biles** A four-wheel vehicle run by an engine: ***Automobiles* are a popular form of transportation around the world.** *syn.* car

ba•lance [bal′əns] *n.* A condition of equality between amounts or values: **When the objects on both sides of a scale have the same weight, they are in *balance*.** *syn.* equality

bar•rel [bar′əl] *n.* A round container, usually made of wood, that is larger around its middle than at its flat top and base: **The *barrel* was filled with water.** *syn.* container

beach [bēch] *n.* The shore of an ocean or a river, especially a sandy or pebbly shore: **Every summer I go to the *beach* with my cousins.** *syns.* coast, shore

beach

bean [bēn] *n.* **beans** The seed of certain plants, used as food: **Rice and *beans* is a popular dish in many countries.**

be•lief [bi•lēf′] *n.* **beliefs** Something thought to be true: **Every religious group has its own set of *beliefs*.** *syn.* faith

beans

blend [blend] *v.* To combine or mix two or more things to make something new: **If you *blend* yellow and red paint, you will have orange paint.** *syns.* mix, combine

branch [branch] *n.* **branch•es** A woody part of a tree, growing out from the trunk: **My uncle hung the swing from one of the tree's highest *branches.***

brave [brāv] *adj.* Having or showing courage: **George Washington was a *brave* soldier.** *syns.* courageous, bold

breathe [brē#h] *v.* To draw air into and let it out from the lungs: **Animals with lungs must *breathe* air to stay alive.**

bro•ken [brō′kən] *adj.* Smashed into pieces or not usable: **My dad is going to take the *broken* bicycle to the repair shop.**

build [bild] *v.* **build•ing** To make something by putting parts or materials together: ***Building* a ship is not easy.** *syns.* construct, make

bur•row [bûr′ō] *n.* A hole made in the ground by certain animals: **A rabbit lives in a *burrow.*** *syns.* hole, tunnel

burrow

busi•ness [biz′nis] *n.* A company formed to make or sell goods or services: **My uncle sells shirts in his clothing *business.*** *syn.* industry

cab•bage [kab′ij] *n.* A vegetable with closely folded leaves forming a hard, round head: **Gabriel ate stuffed *cabbage* for lunch.**

cabbage

cat•tle [kat′əl] *n.* Cows and bulls raised for their milk or meat: **Texas has many ranches that raise *cattle.*** *syn.* livestock

cattle

cen•tu•ry [sen′chə•rē] *n.* A period of 100 years: **The twentieth *century* was a time of many important inventions.**

chore [chôr] *n.* **chores** A job that must be done regularly: **Walking the dog is one of my favorite *chores.*** *syns.* task, job

ci•ty [sit′ē] *n.* A large town with many people: **This *city* has many tall buildings.** *syn.* metropolis

city

cli•mate [klī′mit] *n.* **cli•mates** The kind of weather a place usually has over a long period: **Florida has a warm *climate.*** *syn.* weather

col•o•ny [kol′ə•nē] *n.* **col•o•nies** A piece of land where a group of people settle and remain under the control of the country they came from: **Virginia was one of the British *colonies.*** *syn.* settlement

com•mu•ni•cate [kə•myōō′nə•kāt′] *v.* To share information or ideas: **Telephones make it easier to *communicate* with people who are far away.** *syns.* talk, speak

com•mu•ni•ty [kə•myoo′nə•tē] *n.* A place and the people or animals that live there: **Kansas has a large rural *community*.** *syns.* society, neighborhood

com•pare [kəm•pâr′] *v.* To look at more than one thing and notice how they are the same and how they are different: ***Compare* these two books and tell me which one you like better.** *syn.* contrast

com•pe•ti•tion [kom′pə•tish′ən] *n.* The effort made by two or more people to get the same thing or to be the best: **Do you think all the *competition* among students is good?**

con•struc•tion [kən•struk′shən] *n.* The building of something: **The *construction* of a house takes a long time.** *syn.* building

construction

con•trast [kən•trast′] *v.* To compare two things to show how they are different: ***Contrast* city life with country life.**

con•trol [kən•trōl′] *v.* **con•trols** To direct or manage something or someone: **A police officer sometimes *controls* traffic.** *syn.* direct, command

con•ver•sa•tion [kon′vər•sā′shən] *n.* A sharing of ideas by talking together: **Yesterday Maria and Mr. Garcia had a long *conversation* about their hobbies.** *syn.* talk

co•op•er•ate [kō•op′ə•rāt] *v.* To work with others to do something: **The fourth and fifth grades will *cooperate* to plan the party.**

count•er [koun′tər] *n.* A long board or table, as in a restaurant or store, on which meals are served or goods are sold: **The magazines are on the *counter* at the checkout.**

coun•try [kun′trē] *n.* An area of land with its own people and government: **Every *country* has a flag.** *syn.* nation

country

craft [kraft] *n.* **crafts** Work in which a special skill is used to make things by hand: **Making pottery is one of my mom's favorite *crafts*.** *syns.* art, handiwork

cre•ate [krē•āt′] *v.* To think up and make: **I'd like to *create* a machine that would make my bed every morning.** *syns.* invent, build, make

craft

crea•ture [krē′chər] *n.* **crea•tures** A living thing that is an animal: **Parrots are jungle *creatures*.** *syns.* being, animal

crew [kroo] *n.* A group of people working together to do a job: **Columbus and his *crew* sailed across the Atlantic Ocean.** *syns.* band, group

crop [krop] *n.* **crops** A plant grown for personal use or for sale: **Corn and soybeans are important *crops* in the Midwest.**

crop

cy•cle [sī′kəl] *n.* The stages in the growth of a plant or an animal: **Each animal follows the *cycle* of life of its own kind.**

dan•ger [dān′jər] *n.* A situation that is not safe: **A firefighter's job is full of *danger*.** *syns.* hazard, peril

dar•ing [dâr′ing] *adj.* Brave and adventurous, not afraid of anything: **You have to be a *daring* person to climb a mountain.** *syns.* brave, adventurous, fearless

de•liv•er•y [di•liv′ə•rē] *n.* The taking and handing over of something: **I made the newspaper *delivery* on my bike.**

des•ert [dez′ərt] *n.* A very dry region, often covered with sand, where few or no plants grow: **It is hard to find food or water in a** *desert.*

desert

de•ter•mined [di•tûr′mind] *adj.* Firmly decided about doing something: **Angela was** *determined* **to be the fastest runner in school.**

de•vice [di•vīs′] *n.* **de•vi•ces** An object built for a certain purpose: **Thermometers are** *devices* **for measuring temperature.** *syns.* tool, instrument

dis•co•ver [dis•kuv′ər] *v.* To find or to find out something: **I like to travel and** *discover* **new places.** *syns.* find out, learn about, come across

dis•tance [dis′təns] *n.* The amount of space between two points: **What is the** *distance* **in miles between New York and Chicago?**

di•vide [di•vīd′] *v.* To cut or break into parts: **If we** *divide* **the cake, we can all have some.** *syns.* split, separate

dune [dōōn] *n.* **dunes** A hill or bank of loose sand: **In Florida there are beaches with white, sandy** *dunes.* *syns.* hill, mound

Earth [ûrth] *n.* The planet on which we live; the third planet from the sun: **The** *Earth* **travels around the sun.** *syns.* world, globe

edge [ej] *n.* The line or place where an object or area ends: **You must stand away from the** *edge* **of the train platform.**

Earth

ef•fi•cient [i•fish′ənt] *adj.* Producing results with the least effort or waste: **This is an** *efficient* **machine because it uses little power to do the work.** *syns.* useful, effective

eld•est [el′dist] *adj.* The oldest one in a group: **Joshua is the** *eldest* **cousin, and I am the youngest.** *syn.* oldest

el•e•ment [el′ə•mənt] *n.* **el•e•ments** One of the basic parts of something: **Flour and sugar are two** *elements* **of a cake.** *syns.* component, factor, member

en•e•my [en′ə•mē] *n.* **enemies** An animal, person, nation, or group that tries to harm, destroy, or defeat another: **The cat and the mouse are** *enemies.* *syns.* foe, opponent

en•er•gy [en′ər•jē] *n.* Power from electricity, the sun, or another source: **All beings need** *energy* **to survive.** *syns.* power, force

en•vi•ron•ment [in•vī′rən•mənt] *n.* Everything around a person, animal, or plant: **Cactuses grow well in a desert** *environment.* *syn.* surroundings

environment

ex•er•cise [ek′sər•sīz′] *v.* To develop the body by being active: **When I** *exercise* **every day, I feel well and strong.** *syns.* work out, train

ex•plo•ra•tion [ek′splə•rā′shən] *n.* Traveling through a new region to learn what it is like: **The fifteenth century was a time of great** *exploration.* *syns.* discovery, research

farm•er [fär′mər] *n.* A person who works on or owns a farm: **The** *farmer* **raised chickens, pigs, and cattle.** *syn.* grower

fau•cet [fô′sət] *n.* A device used to control the flow of a liquid from a pipe: **Turn on the** *faucet* **if you want to take a bath.** *syn.* tap

faucet

fig•ure [fig′yər] *n.* **fig•ures** An outline, shape, or form: **Grandma made animal *figures* out of dough.**

fire•place [fīr′plās′] *n.* An opening in which a fire is built indoors, connected with a chimney to let the smoke go outdoors: **In the winter, the family sat around the *fireplace* to stay warm.** *syn.* hearth

flight [flīt] *n.* A trip in an aircraft: **The *flight* from New Delhi to Rome took 18 hours!**

flight

flood [flud] *v.* To cover with water an area not usually covered with it: **If the dam breaks, the river will *flood* the town.** *syn.* swamp

fly•er [flī′ər] *n.* A sheet of paper with information on it: **My sister made a *flyer* about our garage sale next week.** *syns.* leaflet, pamphlet

for•est [fôr′ist] *n.* A thick growth of trees spreading over a large area of land: **The *forest* near my town has many oak trees.** *syn.* woods

forest

frac•tion [frak′shən] *n.* **frac•tions** A number that is more than 0 but less than 1: ***Fractions* show a part of something.**

Word Origins
fraction The word *fraction* comes from the Latin verb *frangere*, meaning "to break." Fractions name the parts of objects or groups that have been "broken" into equal parts.

free•dom [frē′dəm] *n.* The right to do certain things without the control of others: **In the United States, people have the *freedom* to say and write what they think.** *syn.* liberty

gen•er•a•tion [jen′ə•rā′shən] *n.* One step in the line from parent to child to grandchild: **Traditions are passed down from one *generation* to the next.**

goal [gōl] *n.* Something a person wants to do or become: **What is your main *goal* in life?** *syns.* objective, aim

goat [gōt] *n.* An animal, related to the sheep, that has horns, a little beard, and a short tail: **Last summer Gopal went to a farm and learned how to milk a *goat*.**

goat

goods [gŏŏdz] *n. pl.* Objects made to be sold: **You can buy *goods* at a store.** *syn.* products

grand•fa•ther [grand′fä′thər] *n.* The father of one's father or mother: **Ning's *grandfather* lives in China.**

grav•i•ty [grav′ə•tē] *n.* The force that pulls objects toward the center of a planet and keeps them from floating into space: **There is less *gravity* on the Moon than there is on Earth.** *syn.* pull

graze [grāz] *v.* To feed on grass: **The farmer's cattle *graze* in the field.**

hatch [hach] *v.* To come out of an egg, as do birds, insects, and some other animals: **Chicks *hatch* from eggs.**

high•way [hī′wā′] *n.* A main road: **If you want to get there faster, take the *highway*.** *syn.* freeway

highway

ho•ri•zon [hə•rī′zən] *n.* The line where the earth and sky seem to meet: **In the evening, you can see the sun setting on the *horizon*.**

house [hous] *n.* A building for people to live in: **Esther and her brothers live in a big *house* by the train station.** *syn.* home

hun•gry [hung′grē] *adj.* Wanting or needing food: **If you are *hungry*, eat an apple.**

hungry

im•age [im′ij] *n.* **im•a•ges** A picture: **When you turn on the television, *images* appear on the screen.**

im•ag•i•na•tion [i•maj′•ə•nā′shən] *n.* The power to picture something in the mind: **Use your *imagination* to write an interesting story.**

im•mi•grate [im′ə•grāt′] *v.* **im•mi•grat•ed** To come to a country to live there: **My parents *immigrated* to the United States in 1993.**

im•pres•sion [im•presh′ən] *n.* A feeling or idea: **My *impression* is that your sister likes me.** *syn.* feeling

im•prove [im•prōōv′] *v.* To make something better: **Carmakers want to *improve* the quality of their automobiles.**

in•de•pen•dence [in′di•pen′dəns] *n.* Freedom from the control of others: **My bicycle gives me a feeling of *independence* because it lets me go farther.** *syns.* freedom, liberty

in•dus•try [in′də•strē] *n.* **in•dus•tries** Any kind of business: **There are many *industries* in the United States.** *syn.* business

industry

in•ter•est•ing [in′tər•es•ting] *adj.* Inviting curiosity and attention: **I think that history is a very *interesting* subject.**

in•vent [in•vent′] *v.* To think up and make something for the first time: **Thomas Edison loved to *invent* things that made life easier.** *syn.* create

is•land [ī′lənd] *n.* A piece of land, smaller than a continent, that has water all around it: **The *island* of Hawaii has beautiful beaches.**

island

lab•o•ra•to•ry [lab′rə•tôr′ē] *n.* A building or room set up for doing experiments: **Please take these test tubes and charts to the *laboratory*.**

lan•guage [lang′gwij] *n.* The words that the people of a certain nation or group use in speaking and writing: **French is the *language* spoken in France.**

Word Origins
language The word *language* comes from the Latin word *lingua,* which means "tongue." You certainly use your tongue to speak a language!

lead•er [lē′dər] *n.* A person who goes ahead of or directs a group: **Mohammed is the *leader* of the marching band.** *syns.* boss, director

leaf [lēf] *n.* **leaves** One of the flat, thin, usually green parts of a plant: **The dead *leaves* fell from the tree.**

leaf

leave [lēv] *v.* **leav•ing** To go from a place: **Tomás is *leaving* next week on a vacation.** *syns.* depart, go

les•son [les'ən] *n.* An experience from which something can be learned: **I learned my *lesson* when I failed the test because I hadn't studied.** *syn.* moral

lose [lo͞oz] *v.* To be defeated or to fail to win: **Nobody likes to *lose* a game.** *syn.* fail

mam•mal [mam'əl] *n.* A kind of animal of which the females make milk for their young: **A cow is a *mammal*.**

mammal

meal [mēl] *n.* Food served or eaten at a certain time of the day: **In Spain, lunch is the main *meal* of the day.**

mer•chant [mûr'chənt] *n.* **mer•chants** A person who buys and sells things: **The *merchants* bought rugs in India and sold them in England.** *syns.* trader, dealer, retailer

mood [mo͞od] *n.* A way of feeling: **After her team won the game, Helen was in a good *mood*.** *syn.* humor

Moon [mo͞on] *n.* A large natural satellite of Earth: **Do you think that humans will live on the *Moon* one day?**

Moon

moun•tain [moun'tən] *n.* **moun•tains** A landform that is higher than a hill and rises far above the nearby land: **Someday I'll be able to climb those *mountains*.**

name [nām] *n.* A word or group of words by which a person, animal, place, or thing is called: **My *name* is Carl. What is your *name*?**

neigh•bor [nā'bər] *n.* **neigh•bors** A person who lives nearby: **My next-door *neighbors* have a dog.**

neigh•bor•hood [nā'bər•ho͝od'] *n.* A part of a city or town, having homes and usually stores and other services: **There is a big park in my *neighborhood*.** *syn.* community

ner•vous [nûr'vəs] *adj.* Showing worry or fear about something: **I am *nervous* about going to a new school.** *syns.* anxious, worried

nurse [nûrs] *n.* A person who is trained to care for sick, injured, or old people, often in a hospital or nursing home: **The *nurse* bandaged the cut on my arm.**

nurse

nu•tri•tious [no͞o•trish'əs] *adj.* Containing something that is needed by people and animals to stay healthy and strong: **Soybeans are very *nutritious* because they have a lot of protein for growth.** *syns.* nourishing, healthful

o•cean [ō'shən] *n.* The great body of salt water that covers about 70 percent of Earth: **Huge whales live in the *ocean*.** *syn.* sea

ocean

op•por•tu•ni•ty [op′ər•tōō′nə•tē] *n.*
op•por•tu•ni•ties A good chance to do
something: **People often move to places where
there are more *opportunities* for a better life.**
syns. occasion, chance

or•chard [ôr′chərd] *n.* A large group of trees,
planted in order to harvest their fruits: **My
neighbor has an *orchard* of cherry trees.**

ox•y•gen [ok′sə•jin] *n.* A gas that makes up
about one fifth of Earth's atmosphere: **Animals
need *oxygen* to live.**

pa•rade [pə•rād′] *n.* A march that is held as a
celebration: **I love the costumes people wear in
the West Indian *parade*.** *syn.* march

par•a•site [pâr′ə•sīt′] *n.* **par•a•sites** A plant or
animal that gets its food and often its shelter by
living on another plant or animal: **Fleas are
parasites that can live on dogs.**

par•ent [pâr′ənt] *n.* **par•ents** A father or a
mother: **When *parents* cannot care for a child,
another adult will help.** *syns.* mother, father

pen•cil [pen′səl] *n.* **pen•cils** A tool
that has a stick of writing material
inside a covering of wood,
plastic, or metal: **I like
to write with *pencils*
more than with pens.**

pencil

pep•per [pep′ər] *n.* A spicy seasoning made
from the dried berries of a certain plant: **My dad
likes to put *pepper* on his baked potatoes.**

per•mis•sion [pər•mish′ən] *n.* The permitting
or allowing of something: **You need to bring
written *permission* to go on the field trip.**
syn. consent

pi•lot [pī′lət] *n.*
A person who
flies an aircraft:
**The *pilot* landed
the plane safely.**
syns. aviator, flier

pilot

pitch•er [pich′ər] *n.* A container with a handle and
either a lip or spout, used for holding and pouring
liquids: **The *pitcher* was full of water.** *syn.* jug

plane [plān] *n.* An airplane:
**The *plane* flew over the
city.** *syns.* airplane, jet

pock•et [pok′it] *n.* A small
pouch sewn into a garment,
for carrying money or
small objects: **Dad keeps
his car keys in his *pocket*.**

plane

pol•lu•tion [pə•lōō′shən] *n.* Harmful materials
that damage the air, water, and soil: **Pollution in
the air we breathe is bad for our health.**

pop•u•la•tion [pop′yə•lā′shən] *n.*
pop•u•la•tions The number of people or animals
living in a certain area: **China and India have
the largest *populations* in the world.**

pot•ter•y [pot′ə•rē] *n.* Objects that are made
from clay and hardened by heat, such as pots:
**We are studying different types of *pottery*
in art class.** *syn.* ceramics

pottery

prai•rie [prâr′ē] *n.* A large area of grassy land
having few or no trees: **The *prairie* looks like a
sea of grass.** *syns.* plain, grassland

pred•a•tor [pred′ə•tər] *n.* **pred•a•tors** An
animal that hunts other animals for food: **Lions
are fierce *predators*.**

pre•pare [pri•pâr′] *v.* To get ready: **We have to
prepare for tomorrow's field trip.** *syns.* plan,
organize

prob•lem [prob′ləm] *n.* **prob•lems** A situation in
which it is difficult to know what to do: **All
problems have solutions.** *syn.* difficulty

proj•ect [proj′ekt] *n.* A task or piece of work:
**Today we started a new *project* about wild
animals.** *syn.* assignment

385

prom•ise [prom′is] *v.* **prom•ised** To give your word that you will do something: **Aniko *promised* to take her niece to the zoo.**

pro•tec•tion [prə•tek′shən] *n.* The keeping of someone or something safe from danger or harm: **Caves provide animals with *protection* from the weather.** *syn.* defense

ques•tion [kwes′chən] *n.* Something that is asked in order to find out something: **You must answer when the teacher asks you a *question*.**

rail•road [rāl′rōd′] *n.* A transportation system made up of all the tracks and trains belonging to one company: **That *railroad* has tracks in six southern states.**

railroad

re•al•is•tic [rē•əl•is′tik] *adj.* Showing things in a lifelike way: **This sculpture is very *realistic*; you can even see the woman's eyelashes.**

re•port•er [ri•pôr′tər] *n.* A person who gathers information and writes articles for a newspaper or for a radio or television station: **The *reporter* spoke about the damage from the hurricane.** *syn.* journalist

rep•tile [rep′tīl′] *n.* **rep•tiles** Any of a large class of cold-blooded, egg-laying animals: **Alligators are large *reptiles*.**

reptile

res•tau•rant [res′tər•ənt] *n.* **res•tau•rants** A place where meals are cooked and served for a price: **I love to eat in new *restaurants*.**

ri•ver [riv′ər] *n.* A large, natural stream of water flowing into the sea, a lake, or another river: **When it is hot, Rita and Claire swim in the *river* near their house.**

river

root [rōōt] *n.* **roots** The part of the plant that grows below the ground and takes up water and food from the soil: **Don't destroy the *roots*, or the tree will die.**

rule [rōōl] *n.* **rules** A direction or a law that tells what one must or must not do: **If you want to play a game with us, you must follow the *rules*.** *syn.* law

rush [rush] *v.* **rushed** To move or go with great speed: **They *rushed* away from the burning building.** *syn.* hurry

safe•ty [sāf′tē] *n.* Freedom from danger or injury: **Nothing is more important to families than the *safety* of their children.**

salt [sôlt] *n.* White crystals obtained from seawater and as a mineral in the earth. Salt can be used to preserve and to season food: **Eva always seasons her salad with *salt* and olive oil.**

salt

Word Origins

salt Long ago, before refrigerators were invented, salt was a very important mineral because it could keep certain foods from spoiling. It was so important that the soldiers of the Roman Empire were paid in salt instead of money. This "salt money" was called *salary*, from the Latin word for *salt*, *sal*.

scarf [skärf] *n.* A band or square of cloth worn around the head, neck, or shoulders for warmth or style: **Rina wore a beautiful silk *scarf* to the dinner party.**

scene [sēn] *n.* **scenes** A certain place and everything in it: **Renoir's paintings show peaceful country *scenes*.** *syns.* picture, landscape, setting

school

school [skool] *n.* A place set up to teach students: **Every day I go to *school* to learn.**

score [skôr] *v.* To make points, as in a game: **The goal of this game is to *score* as many points as possible.** *syn.* make

sea•shore [sē'shôr'] *n.* The land that borders on the ocean: **The hurricane destroyed many homes by the *seashore*.** *syns.* shore, beach, coast

seashore

sea•son [sē'zən] *n.* One of the four parts of the year—spring, summer, fall, and winter: **Summer is my favorite *season* because I like the warm weather.** *syns.* period, time

set•tle [set'əl] *v.* **set•tled** To make a home in a place: **The early pioneers *settled* along the East coast.**

share [shâr] *v.* **shar•ing** To offer one's things or ideas: ***Sharing* is very important in a friendship.** *syns.* split, divide

shocked [shokt] *adj.* Surprised, horrified, or disgusted by something or someone: **Kato was *shocked* by the sad news.** *syn.* stunned

so•lu•tion [sə•loo'shən] *n.* The answer to a problem: **Have you found the *solution* to your problem?** *syn.* answer

solve [solv] *v.* To find or to work out the answer or solution to a problem: **He liked to *solve* difficult riddles.** *syn.* resolve

space•ship [spās'ship'] *n.* The science fiction word for a vehicle used for travel in space: **In the movie, a *spaceship* from Mars landed on Earth.** *syn.* spacecraft

spe•cial [spesh'əl] *adj.* Of an unusual kind; not ordinary: **This weekend I want to do something *special* for my aunt because it's her birthday.** *syns.* particular, unusual

speech [spēch] *n.* Words that are spoken, especially as a talk to an audience: **The audience clapped when he finished his *speech*.**

sport [spôrt] *n.* **sports** A game or a contest that takes athletic skill— for example, baseball, football, or track: **One of my favorite winter *sports* is ice hockey.** *syn.* game

sport

state [stāt] *n.* In a country, a section that has its own government: **Brooklyn is located in the *state* of New York.**

street [strēt] *n.* **streets** A public road in a city or town, usually with sidewalks and buildings on one or both sides: **There is a new movie theater a few *streets* from my house.** *syns.* road, lane, avenue

street

strong [strông] *adj.* Having great strength or ability: **Claudia is very *strong* in math.** *syns.* capable, competent

suc•cess [sək•ses′] *n.* A good outcome: **The concert was a *success*; everybody loved it.** *syns.* achievement, accomplishment

su•per•mar•ket [soo′pər•mär′kit] *n.* A large grocery store in which customers select goods from the shelves and pay as they leave: **Once a week, my dad goes to the *supermarket* to buy food.** *syn.* grocery store

supermarket

sup•per [sup′ər] *n.* An evening meal; the last meal of the day: **Tonight we'll have soup and salad for *supper*.** *syn.* dinner

sur•face [sûr′fis] *n.* The outer part of something: **There isn't any water on the *surface* of the Moon.** *syn.* covering

sur•viv•al [sər•vī′vəl] *n.* Remaining alive through a dangerous event: **Clean water is important for the *survival* of sea animals.** *syns.* subsistence, endurance

taste [tāst] *n.* The flavor of a food: **Jeremy loves the *taste* of spicy food.** *syn.* flavor

teach•er [tē′chər] *n.* A person who gives lessons: **The *teacher* asked me to read the poem.** *syns.* instructor, professor

team [tēm] *n.* A group of people who work or play together: **My sister plays on a basketball *team*.** *syns.* group, band

team

team•work [tēm′wûrk′] *n.* The working together of a team or group to reach a goal: **In baseball, you need *teamwork* to win.** *syn.* cooperation

teamwork

tem•per•a•ture [tem′pər•ə•chər] *n.* The degree of heat or cold in a body or thing: **The *temperature* in the mountains is usually lower than in the valley.**

temperature

ter•ri•to•ry [ter′ə•tôr′ē] *n.* Any large area of land: **Pioneers traveled to unknown *territory*.** *syns.* region, area

thirst•y [thûrs′tē] *adj.* Having a feeling of dryness in the mouth and throat caused by a need to drink: **I am very *thirsty*; may I have some juice, please?**

to•geth•er [tə•geth′ər] *adv.* With one another: **Shawn and Rasheed built the model plane *together*.** *syns.* jointly, collectively

tour•ist [toor′ist] *n.* **tourists** A person who travels for pleasure: **The *tourists* took a picture of the monument.** *syns.* traveler, visitor

trade [trād] *n.* A kind of work that requires training and usually working with the hands or with machines: **Ahmed is a tailor by *trade*.** *syns.* occupation, profession

tra•di•tion [trə•dish′ən] *n.* **traditions** A custom, belief, or idea that is passed from one generation to the next: **Quilting is one of my family's *traditions*.** *syns.* custom, ritual

train [trān] *n.* A line of railway cars that are joined: **The *train* to Rome was full of passengers.**

train

trans•por•ta•tion [trans′pər•tā′shən] *n.* The moving of things or people from one place to another: **The subway is a convenient form of *transportation* in New York City.**

trav•el [trav′əl] *v.* To go from one place to another: **I love to *travel* by train because trains are fast and comfortable.**

trip [trip] *n.* A journey or a voyage: **Next year we'll take a *trip* to the mountains.** *syns.* voyage, expedition, excursion, journey

va•ca•tion [vā•kā′shən] *n.* A time for rest and enjoyment: **Next summer Lisa and Heidi will go to Nepal on *vacation.* ** *syn.* holiday

vis•it [viz′it] *v.* To go to see people or places, or to stay with a person or in a place as a guest: **Every winter I go with my parents to *visit* my aunt and uncle in Idaho.**

wag•on [wag′ən] *n.* A large vehicle pulled by animals and used mainly to carry goods: **The horses pulled the *wagon.* ** *syns.* carriage, cart

wagon

warn [wôrn] *v.* **warned** To tell of possible harm or danger: **My cousin *warned* us about her dog.** *syns.* caution, advise

wa•ter [wôt′ər] *n.* The transparent liquid that falls from the clouds as rain and fills oceans, rivers, and lakes: **If you are thirsty, you should drink a glass of *water.* **

wa•ter•way [wô′tər•wā′] *n.* **wa•ter•ways** A body of water, such as a river or canal, used for travel: **The ship traveled through many *waterways* on its way to Chicago.**

waterway

win [win] *v.* To be successful in a game, contest, war, or other struggle: **If we *win* this game, we'll play in the state championship.**

wor•ried [wûr′ēd] *adj.* Feeling uneasy and anxious: **I am *worried* about my cousin because it's one o'clock and she hasn't arrived yet.** *syns.* anxious, distressed, fearful

Word Origins
worried Do you ever feel your worries are "strangling" you? In Old English, *worry* was spelled *wyrgan,* and it meant "to strangle."

Index of Titles and Authors

Acknowledgments

For permission to reprint copyrighted material, grateful acknowledgment is made to the following sources:

Aladdin Paperbacks, an imprint of Simon & Schuster Children's Publishing Division: Someplace Else by Carol P. Saul, illustrated by Barry Root. Text copyright © 1995 by Carol P. Saul; illustrations copyright © 1995 Barrett Root.

Charlesbridge Publishing Inc.: From *Let the Games Begin!* by Maya Ajmera and Michael J. Regan. Text copyright © 2000 by SHAKTI for Children.

Cobblehill Books, an affiliate of Dutton Children's Books, an imprint of Penguin Putnam Books for Young Readers, a division of Penguin Putnam, Inc.: From *Nature's Great Balancing Act: In Our Own Backyard* by E. Jaediker Norsgaard, photographs by Campbell Norsgaard. Text copyright © 1990 by E. Jaediker Norsgaard; photographs copyright © 1990 by Campbell Norsgaard.

Harcourt, Inc.: From *Weird Friends: Unlikely Allies in the Animal Kingdom* by Jose Aruego and Ariane Dewey. Copyright © 2000 by Jose Aruego and Ariane Dewey.

HarperCollins Publishers: Grandpa's Corner Store by DyAnne DiSalvo-Ryan. Copyright © 2000 by DyAnne DiSalvo-Ryan. From *Stories to Solve: Folktales from Around the World* by George Shannon, illustrated by Peter Sís. Text copyright © 1985 by George Shannon; illustrations copyright © 1985 Peter Sís.

Holiday House, Inc.: From *Pueblo Storyteller* by Diane Hoyt-Goldsmith, photographs by Lawrence Migdale. Text copyright © 1991 by Diane Hoyt-Goldsmith; photographs copyright © 1991 by Lawrence Migdale.

Houghton Mifflin Company: When Jo Louis Won the Title by Belinda Rochelle, illustrated by Larry Johnson. Text copyright © 1994 by Belinda Rochelle; illustrations copyright © 1994 by Larry Johnson.

M. Donnaleen Howitt: "Me-First Millie" by M. Donnaleen Howitt from *U. S. Kids, a Weekly Reader* Magazine, December 1990.

Kingfisher Publications plc: From *Our Universe: A Guide to What's Out There* (Retitled: "Journey Through the Solar System") by Russell Stannard, illustrated by Michael Bennallack-Hart, Helen Floate, and Diana Mayo. Text copyright © 1995 by Russell Stannard; illustrations copyright © 1995 by Larousse plc.

Scholastic Inc.: Amelia and Eleanor Go for a Ride by Pam Muñoz Ryan, illustrated by Brian Selznick. Text copyright © 1999 by Pam Muñoz Ryan; illustrations copyright © 1999 by Brian Selznick. Published by Scholastic Press, a division of Scholastic Inc.

SPIDER Magazine: "Spider Soup," adapted by Phillis Gershator from *Spider* Magazine, Vol. 2, No. 6. Text copyright © 1995 by Phillis Gershator.

Photo Credits

Page Placement Key: (t)-top (c)-center (b)-bottom (l)-left (r)-right (fg)-foreground (bg)-background

8 Michael S. Yamashita/Corbis; 9 Harcourt; 10 Harcourt; 11 David Muench/Corbis; 12-18 Harcourt; 19 (tl) LWA - Dann Tardif/Corbis; 19 (tr) (br) Harcourt; 19 (bl) Danny Lehman/Corbis; 22-32 Harcourt; 33 (t) S. Piumatti/H. Armstrong Roberts; 35 (r) Harcourt; 35-36 (b) Royalty-Free/Corbis; 36 (tl) (tr) Harcourt; 36 (br) S. Meltzer/PhotoLink/Getty Images; 37 (tl) (tr) (br) Harcourt; 38 (t) PictureNet/Corbis, 39 (l) (u) (br) Harcourt; (bl) Howard Davies/Corbis; 44 (t) Harcourt; 45 (tl) (tr) (br) Harcourt; (bl) Royalty-Free/Corbis; 62-63 (c) Harcourt; (r) (b) Harcourt; 63 (t) Michelle D. Bridwell/PhotoEdit; (b) Harcourt; 64 Weronica Ankarorn/Harcourt; 66-69 Weronica Ankarorn/Harcourt; 76 (t) (b) Harcourt; 77 (tl) (tr) (b) Harcourt; (bc) Gunter Marx Photography/Corbis; 78-79 Ken Kinzie/Harcourt; 80 (l) Gary Retherford/Science Source/Photo Researchers; (r) Sinclair Stammers/Science Photo Library/Photo Researchers; (b) Harcourt; 81 HaKen Kinzie/Harcourt; 82 (t) PictureNet/Corbis 83-96 Harcourt; 97 (t) R.W. Jones/Corbis; (tr) (br) Harcourt; (bl) Bohemian Nomad Picturemakers/Corbis; 98 Royalty-Free/Corbis; 99 (t) Nancie Battaglia; (b) Nik Wheeler; (br) Kevin R. Morris/Corbis; 100-101 (c) Duomo/Corbis; 100 (tl) Nik Wheeler; (bl) AFP/Corbis; 101 (t) Mary Altier; (b) Bob Daemmrich/The Image Works; 102 (t) David Alan Harvey/Woodfin Camp & Associates; (b) Debbie Simerlink; 103 (t) Nik Wheeler; (b) Amateur Athletic Foundation; 104 (tl) Michael J. Doolittle/The Image Works; (br) Eastcott/Momatiuk/Woodfin Camp; 105 (t) Robert Frerck/Woodfin Camp & Associates; (bl) Stephine Maze; (br) Jan Reynolds; 106 Nik Wheeler; 107 (t) Nile Sprague; (b) Nancie Battaglia; 108 (t) Nancie Battaglia; 108-109 (b) Tom Bean/Corbis; 109 (t) M. E. Newman/Woodfin Camp & Associates; (b(inset) Bob Daemmrich/The Image Works; 110 (t) Nancie Battaglia; 110-111 (c) Pete Saloutos/Corbis; 111 (t) Karim Shamsi-Basha; (b) Stefanie Felix; 112 (t) Nancie Battaglia; (b) John D. Ivanko; (b (inset) Dinodia/Mishra; 113 (t) Wolfgang Kaehler; 113 (b) AP/Wide World Photos; 114-115 (c) Ken Kinzle/Harcourt; 114 (t) Harcourt; (bl) Getty Images; (br) Harcourt; 115 (t) Getty Images; (tl) (br) Harcourt; (tr) Getty Images; 128-129 Harcourt; 130 (b) Jay Halaska/Photo Researchers; (tl) (tr) Harcourt; (inset) Alvin E. Staffan/Photo Researchers; 131 (r) Jim Zipp/Photo Researchers; (b) Jan Halaska/Photo Researchers; 132 (t) Jeff Lepore/Photo Researchers; (b) Jan Halaska/Photo Researchers; (tl) Harcourt; 133 (b) Jan Halaska/Photo Researchers; 134-135 (c) Robert C. Hermes/Photo Researchers; 134 (tl) Dr. Eckart Pott/OKAPIA/Photo Researchers; (bl) S. Dimmitt/Photo Researchers; (br) Rich Franco/Harcourt; (br) C Squared Studios/Getty Images; (tl(inset) Harcourt; (bl(inset) Siede Preis/Getty Images; 135 (tr) Andrew Ward/Life File/Getty Images; (br) Joyce Photographics/Photo Researchers; (br(inset) Calvin Larsen/Photo Researchers; (tr(inset) Ken Kinzie/Harcourt; 136-153 Harcourt; 154 (b) Brown Brothers; 154-159 (background) (r) Harcourt; 156 (l) American Stock; 156 (inset) American Stock; 157 (b) Getty Images; 158-159 American Stock; 160 (b) Stephen F. Rich/Oregon Trail Regional Museum, Baker City, Oregon; (tl) Victoria Bowen/Harcourt; (tr) Steve Yeater/Black Star/Harcourt; 161 (t) Weronica Ankarorn/Harcourt; (b) Bob Daemmrich Photography; 162 -163 Harcourt; 188 (t) Paul Almasy/Corbis; (b) Harcourt; 189 (tl) Michael Dunne/Elizabeth Whiting & Associates/Corbis; (tr) (bl) Harcourt; (br) Gail Mooney/Corbis; 190-197 Lawrence Migdale; 198 (c) The Newark Museum/Art Resource, NY; (tr) Superstock; (bl) Cummer Museum of Art and Gardens/Superstock; 199 (tr) Bly Photography; (br) Aldo Tutino/Art Resource, NY; 200 (t) Gerrit Greve/Corbis; (bl) Burstein Collection/Corbis; 201 (t) Craig Tuttle/Corbis; (bl) John Henley/Corbis; (br) Albright-Knox Art Gallery/Corbis; 202 Superstock Inc. Collection, Jacksonville/Superstock; 203 Superstock; 204 (tl) Superstock Inc. Collection, Jacksonville/ Superstock (Detail); (tr) Superstock (Detail); (bl) Superstock Inc. Collection, Jacksonville/Superstock (Detail); (br) Superstock (Detail); (cl) Superstock Inc. Collection., Jacksonville/Superstock (Detail); (cr) Superstock (Detail); 206 (t) Niall Benvie/Corbis; (b) Laura Dwight/Corbis; 207 Harcourt; 224 (t) Royalty-Free/Corbis; (b) Neil Rabinowitz/Corbis; 225 (tl) Jeffrey Coolidge/Corbis; (tr) Harcourt; (bl) Royalty-Free/Corbis; (br) Harcourt; 226 (t) Bettmann/Corbis; 226-227 (c) U.S. Department of the Interior/National Park Service/Edison National Historic Site; 226 (b) National Portrait Gallery; 227 (t) Michael Freeman/Corbis; (b) Getty Images; 228 (t) Harcourt; 228 (t) Getty Images; 229 (r) Getty Images; 229 (b) (bl) Harcourt; 230 U.S. Department of the Interior/National Park Service/ Edison National Historic Site; 231 (t) Harcourt; 231 (b) Bettmann/Corbis; 232 (inset) Brian Minnich/Harcourt; 232-232 Brian Minnich/Harcourt; 233 (inset) Brian Minnich/Harcourt; 234 Brian Minnich/Harcourt; 235-239 (b) Brian Minnich/Harcourt; 244 (t) Harcourt; 244 (b) Royalty-Free/Corbis; 245 (tl) Joseph Sohm; ChromoSohm Inc./Corbis; (tr) Harcourt; (bl) Royalty-Free/Corbis; (br) Corbis; 246 The Granger Collection(detail); 247 (t) Independence National Historical Park; 248 (t) North Wind Pictures Archives; (b) The Granger Collection; 250-251 Harcourt; 252-253 (t) Index Stock Photography; 253 (b) Mark Richards/PhotoEdit; 254 (t) Morton Beebe/Corbis; (b) Harcourt; 255 (t) Gibson Stock Photography; (b) Panoramic Images; 256-285 Ken Kinzie/Harcourt; 286-289 Campbell Norsgaard/Newcombe Productions; 290 Herb Segars/Animals Animals; 292 Stephen Dalton/Photo Researchers; 293 Art Wolfe/Stone/Getty Images; 294 Dwight Kuhn/Bruce Coleman, Inc.; 295 (b) E. R. Degginger/Animals Animals; Laura Riley/Bruce Coleman, Inc.; 296-297 W. Bayer/Bruce Coleman, Inc.; 298 S. Nielsen/Bruce Coleman, Inc.; 299 (t) Joe McDonald/Animals Animals; (b) Laura Riley/Bruce Coleman, Inc.; 300 (l) Phil Degginger/Bruce Coleman, Inc.; (r) Keith Gunnar/Bruce Coleman, Inc.; 301 Robert P. Carr/Bruce Coleman, Inc.; 314-315 Harcourt; 316 (u) Corbis; (bl) Getty Images; 317 (tr) Underwood Photo Archives/Superstock; (bl) Duke University; 318-319 (t) Superstock; 318 (bl) Index Stock Photography; 319 (r) NASA; 320-321 (c) NASA; 320 (b) Harcourt; (tl) Getty Images; 321 (t) Alan and Sandy Carey/Getty Images; (b) Harcourt; 322 -339 Harcourt; 340-341 (c) NASA; 341 -353 NASA; 358-359 Harcourt. Page 378(tl), Digital Stock; 378(bl), 378(tr), 378(br), Harcourt Index; 379(tl), Harcourt Telescope; 379(bl), 379(tr), 379(br), 380(l), Harcourt Index; 381(tr), Harcourt Telescope; 381(br), Harcourt Index; 381(tl), Harcourt Telescope; 381(bl), Harcourt Index; 381(tr), Harcourt Telescope; 381(br), 382(tl), Harcourt Index; 382(bl), 382(tr), Harcourt Telescope; 382(br), 383(tl), 383(bl), 383(tr), 383(br), Harcourt Index; 384(tl), Harcourt Telescope; 384(bl), 384(tr), 384(br), 385(tl), Harcourt Telescope; 385(bl), Comstock.com; 385(tl), Corel; 385(bl), Harcourt Telescope; 386(tl), Harcourt Index; 386(bl), Harcourt Telescope; 386(tr), 386(br), 387(tl), 387(bl), Harcourt Index; 387(tr), Harcourt Telescope; 387(br), Brand X Pictures; 388(tl), 388(bl), 388(tr), 388(br), Harcourt Index; 389(tl), Corel; 389(bl), 389(r), Harcourt Telescope.

Illustration Credits

Adair Pain, 16-17; Jui Ishida, 20-27; Janell Genovese, 40-43; Larry Johnson, 46-63; Dennard, Lacey & Associates, 64-69; Greg Morgan, 74-75; Holly Cooper, 84-87; Cathy Bennett, 90-93; Gerardo Suzan, 116-121; Jui Ishida, 124-125; Elizabeth Brandt, 126-127; Barry Root, 164-175; Christiane Beauregard, 176-181; Katherine Lucas, 186-187; Peter Sís, 208-221; Erika LeBarre, 222-223; Dennard, Lacey & Associates, 232-237; Jon Flaming, 242-243; Will Terry, 302-307; Gerardo Suzan, 310-311; Dennard, Lacey & Associates, 312-313; Brian Selznick, 324-337; Greg Newbold, 356-357; Amy Ning, 360-367; Stephen Quinlan, 368-373.